EYEWITNESS
TRAIN

Jigsaw puzzle featuring
Thomas the Tank Engine

Midland Railway coat of arms

Train
ticket

Model of 1843 Norris
locomotive

Signal box bell
tapper

Preserved 1938 steam locomotive *Duchess of Hamilton*

EYEWITNESS

TRAIN

WRITTEN BY
JOHN COILEY

Metal whistle

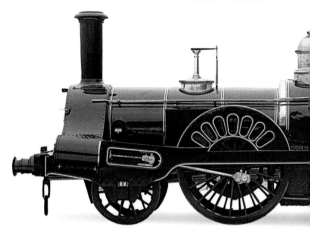

Columbine steam
locomotive, 1845

Railroad police
batons

French rail free pass

DUCHESS OF HAMILTON

Penguin Random House

REVISED EDITION

DK LONDON
Senior Editor Carron Brown
Designer Chrissy Barnard
Senior US Editor Megan Douglass
Managing Editor Francesca Baines
Managing Art Editor Philip Letsu
Production Editor Robert Dunn
Senior Production Controller Jude Crozier
Senior Jackets Designer Surabhi Wadhwa-Gandhi
Jacket Design Development Manager Sophia MTT
Publisher Andrew Macintyre
Associate Publishing Director Liz Wheeler
Art Director Karen Self
Publishing Director Jonathan Metcalf

Consultant Anthony Coulls

DK DELHI
Senior Editor Priyanka Kharbanda
Senior Art Editor Vikas Chauhan
Art Editors Deepshikha Walia, Aparajita Sen
Picture Researcher Vishal Ghavri
Managing Editor Kingshuk Ghoshal
Managing Art Editor Govind Mittal
DTP Designers Pawan Kumar, Rakesh Kumar, Ashok Kumar
Jacket Designer Juhi Sheth

FIRST EDITION
Project Editor Christine Webb **Art Editor** Ann Cannings
Managing Editor Helen Parker **Managing Art Editor** Julia Harris
Production Louise Barratt **Picture Research** Cynthia Hole
Special Photography Mike Dunning

This Eyewitness ® Book has been conceived by
Dorling Kindersley Limited and Editions Gallimard

This American Edition, 2022
First American Edition, 1992
Published in the United States by DK Publishing
1745 Broadway, 20th Floor, New York, NY 10019

A catalog record for this book is available from the Library of Congress.

ISBN 978-0-7440-5642-6 (Paperback)
ISBN 978-0-7440-5644-0 (ALB)

DK books are available at special discounts when
purchased in bulk for sales promotions, premiums,
fund-raising, or educational use. For details, contact:
DK Publishing Special Markets,
1745 Broadway, 20th Floor, New York, NY 10019
SpecialSales@dk.com

Printed and bound in China

For the curious
www.dk.com

This book was made with Forest
Stewardship Council™ certified paper—
one small step in DK's commitment to a
sustainable future. For more information
go to www.dk.com/our-green-pledge

Royal train
headlight

Passenger
tickets

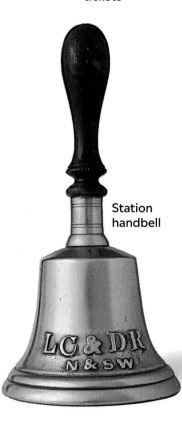

Station
handbell

Late 19th-century
pocket watch

Mechanical
semaphore signal

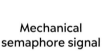

Car keys

Model of
American steam
locomotive, 1875

Contents

Sectioned model of 1829 steam locomotive *Novelty*

What is a **train?**

A train is a series of vehicles on wheels pulled along a railroad track by a locomotive. The earliest trains relied on human power to push or pull them along the tracks. Later, horses could pull heavier loads. But it was the invention of the steam locomotive in the early 1800s that led to the rapid rise of the railroads. The new powerful steam trains could travel at greater speeds. Steam power lasted until the mid-20th century, when it was replaced by diesel engines and electric motors.

Muscle power

The earliest railroads were built in mines to transport coal. To build the longer, public railroads, a huge workforce had to dig and move soil, lay tracks, and build bridges and tunnels using basic hand tools and sheer muscle power.

Passenger trains

In the early 1820s and 1830s, cars in the passenger trains were little more than open wagons with seats (pp. 28–29). Over time, train cars were equipped with lighting, heating, and lavatories. For longer journeys, sleeping and dining cars were available.

Day trippers

Steam trains were a familiar sight by the end of the 19th century. People in rural areas could now travel to the cities for work or pleasure. City dwellers could also enjoy trips to the country or the seaside.

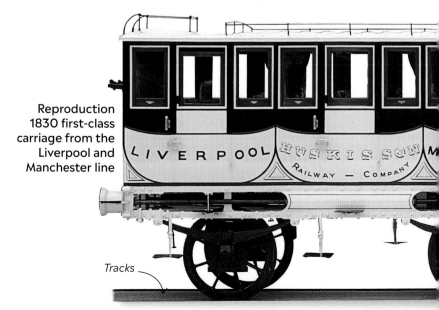

Reproduction 1830 first-class carriage from the Liverpool and Manchester line

Tracks

Electric trains

Electric trains first ran on an underground railroad in the 1890s (pp. 56–57). Powered by overhead cables, or from a live rail on the track, electric trains are faster, quieter, and cleaner than diesel or steam locomotives.

Moving goods

The earliest trains were built to move freight (goods) such as coal (pp. 26–27). Today, railroads remain an important method of moving freight, although traffic in most countries has declined dramatically due to competition from road transportation.

Diesel trains

The first successful passenger diesel trains were introduced in the 1930s in Europe and the US. Today, diesel power is used worldwide (pp. 40–41).

Locomotive power

The first trains, like this modern reproduction, were hauled by steam locomotives. Nowadays, most trains are hauled by diesel or electric locomotives.

Reproduction of Robert Stephenson's *Rocket* locomotive of 1829

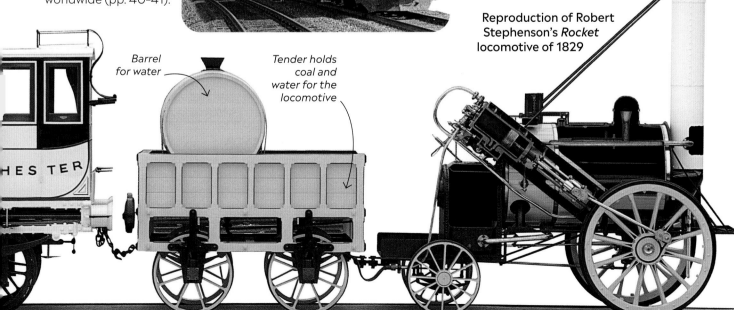

Barrel for water

Tender holds coal and water for the locomotive

HES TER

The first railroads

Railroads existed long before steam engines were invented. Heavy loads were transported in wheeled wagons that ran on parallel wooden planks. Later, railroads had different guiding systems. Some had rails with flanges to stop the wheels from slipping off. Others had smooth rails, with flanged wheels to keep them on the tracks. Before steam trains, heavy loads were transported by either human power or horsepower.

Ancient roadways
Early civilizations, such as the Babylonians and Sumerians, built roadways made out of stone slabs. Because the road surfaces were uneven, grooves were cut into the stone to guide the vehicles. Grooved stone tracks made by the Romans can still be seen in the ruins of Pompeii (above).

Easy rider
Some of the earliest railroads in Britain were used to transport coal from the mines to nearby rivers—a journey that was usually downhill. Horses often traveled down in a wagon called a dandy cart to conserve their energy for the long uphill journey back.

This dandy cart was used to transport a horse downhill.

Stagecoach
The stagecoach was the fastest means of transportation before the railroads. By swapping teams of horses when they tired, stagecoaches and fast mail coaches could travel at an average speed of around 7 mph (11 kph).

Human power
This engraving, published in 1752, was the first illustration of an English railroad. It is also the first recorded use of a flanged wheel on a railroad in Britain.

Heavy loads

This English railroad was built in 1815, and was used for transporting coal. Its rails were made of cast iron. Horses were used to pull the wagons, which were fitted with flanged wheels.

Japanese horsepower

Horse-powered railroads were widely used throughout the world until the early 1900s.

Delivering coal

Loaded coal wagons were rolled downhill to nearby rivers. This brakeman controls the wagon's speed using a simple lever brake, while the horse follows behind.

Early German railroads

Horses had been used on wagon ways in Germany since the 18th century. The first steam railroad in Germany opened in 1835 (see pp. 16–17).

Coal carrier

The wooden wagon used to carry coal in the northeast of England was known as a chaldron. It was loaded from above at the mine. When it arrived at the river, it emptied the coal through a door in the floor directly into the ship waiting below.

A wagonload of coal became a measure known as a "chaldron."

1155 S·H 2·18

Brake lever

Flanged wheel

Dawn of the steam age

Ever since the first practical steam engines were designed by Thomas Newcomen in 1712, and James Watt in 1769, engineers tried to use steam power to drive a self-propelled vehicle. It was not until the early 19th century that the first successful steam locomotives were designed. However, engines had to be powerful enough to pull heavy loads, and make as little noise and smoke as possible. They also had to run on smooth rails that would not break under their weight.

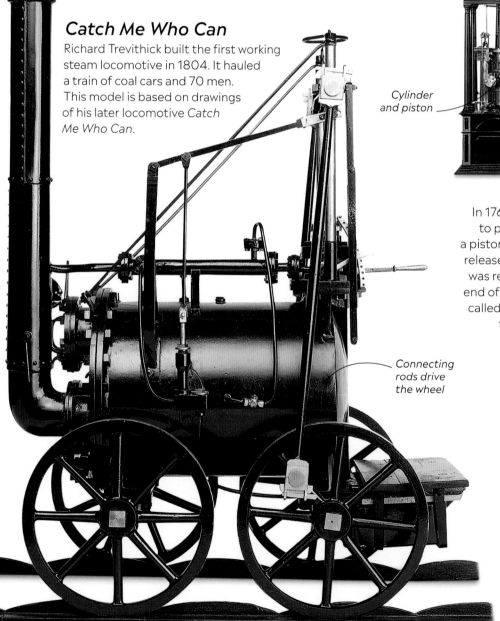

Catch Me Who Can
Richard Trevithick built the first working steam locomotive in 1804. It hauled a train of coal cars and 70 men. This model is based on drawings of his later locomotive *Catch Me Who Can*.

Beam

Flywheel

Cylinder and piston

Watt's steam engine
In 1769, James Watt invented a steam engine to pump water from mines. Steam pushed a piston to the top of a cylinder. When steam was released, the piston moved down, and the cycle was repeated. The piston was attached to one end of a beam, and its other end turned a wheel called a flywheel. This engine was, however, far too big and heavy for a locomotive.

Connecting rods drive the wheel

Local attraction
This engraving shows a steam locomotive built in 1808 by Richard Trevithick. Known as *Catch Me Who Can*, it pulled a four-wheeled car around a circular track.

By land and by water

The first self-propelled land vehicle in America was this scow (a type of boat) built by Oliver Evans in 1804. On land, it ran on wheels under its own steam. When it reached water, the wheels were removed.

Getting a grip

For early locomotives, like the one in this 1812 engraving, engineers had to ensure the wheels could grip the smooth rails. They made the driving wheel fit onto a toothed rack running along the rails.

Chaos

This 1828 cartoon shows what the streets of London, UK, might have looked like with the arrival of steam-powered road vehicles.

Puffing Billy is one of the two oldest surviving steam locomotives in the world.

Puffing Billy

Puffing Billy was built by Englishman William Hedley in 1813 and was used to haul coal wagons. Because of complaints about noise and smoke, *Puffing Billy* was adapted so the steam passed through a "quieting" chamber before going up the chimney.

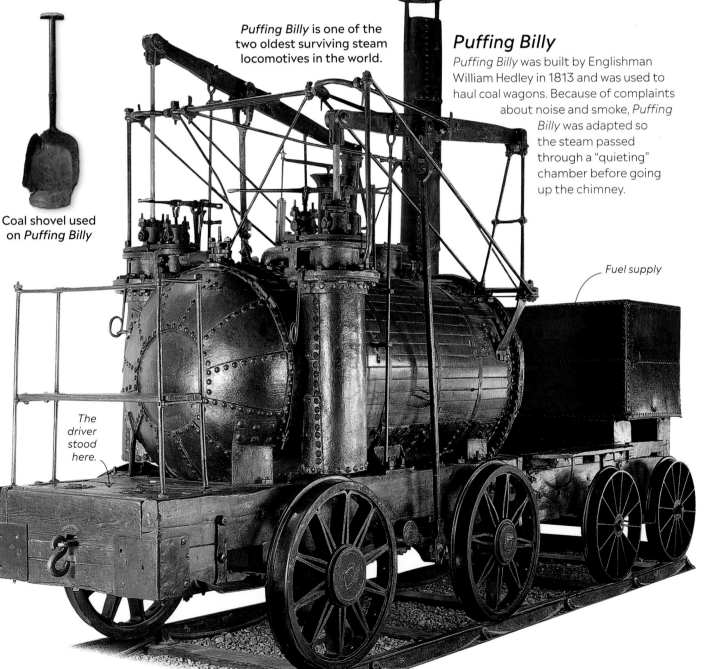

Coal shovel used on *Puffing Billy*

Fuel supply

The driver stood here.

Steam locomotives come of age

It was the vision of British railroad engineer George Stephenson that led the way to the age of steam. Together with his son Robert, Stephenson established his locomotive works in 1823 and began to build steam locomotives for Britain and the world. By the mid-19th century, the steam locomotive had been adopted worldwide as a result of its strength, simplicity, and reliability. The basic principles of the steam locomotive's design remained largely unchanged until diesel-electric and electric locomotives signaled the end of the age of steam.

Best Friend of Charleston
The Best Friend of Charleston was the first successful steam locomotive to be built in the US. It operated a regular steam passenger service from 1830.

Railroad directors were provided with free passes for life, such as this engraved ivory free pass from c. 1830.

Steam for the people
The very first public railroad—the Stockton and Darlington Railway—opened in England in 1825. At first, the locomotives on this line were reserved for freight trains. It was not until 1833 that they were used for passenger trains.

Novelty

In 1829, the Rainhill trials were held to choose a locomotive design for the new Liverpool and Manchester Railway in England. One of the entrants, *Novelty*, was a very fast engine, but it broke down too frequently.

Upright boiler

Sectioned model of *Novelty*

American classics

Steam passenger trains were established in the United States by the mid-19th century. US locomotives had large headlights, wooden "cowcatchers" for sweeping animals off the line, and bronze warning bells.

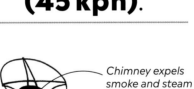

Rocket could hit a top speed of 28 mph (45 kph).

Flying Scotsman

By the 1920s, express trains ran throughout the world. One of the most famous, the *Flying Scotsman*, traveled 393 miles (633 km) between London and Edinburgh, Scotland.

Chimney expels smoke and steam

Winner takes all

Rocket is one of the most famous locomotives in the world. It entered the 1829 Rainhill trials, and won the competition. British engineer Robert Stephenson was largely responsible for the design of *Rocket*.

Polish stamp showing a locomotive built by Robert Stephenson

How a steam locomotive works

American steam locomotive

The design of all steam locomotives is based on the same principles. A coal fire in the firebox heats water in the boiler, producing steam. This steam is used to move a piston back and forth. The movement of the piston turns the wheels through a connecting rod and crank system. In all, it takes about three hours for the locomotive to produce enough steam to move.

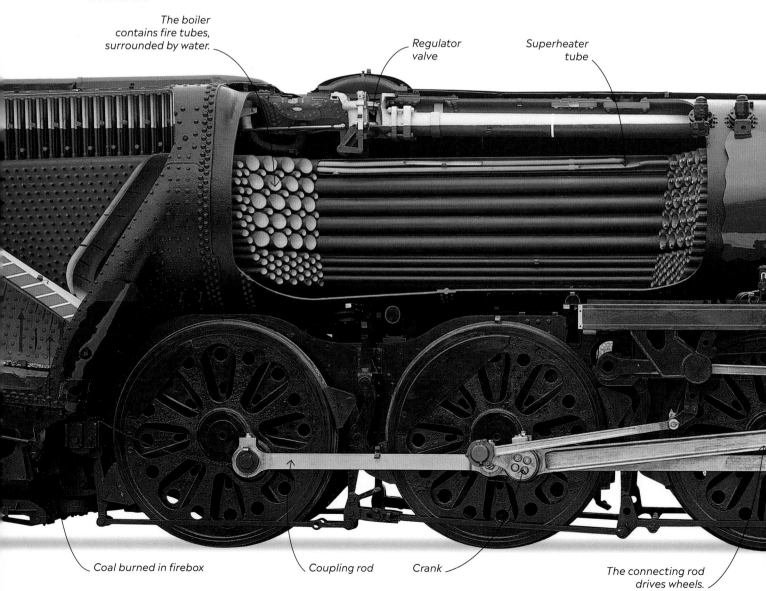

The boiler contains fire tubes, surrounded by water.

Regulator valve

Superheater tube

Coal burned in firebox

Coupling rod

Crank

The connecting rod drives wheels.

Inside the cab

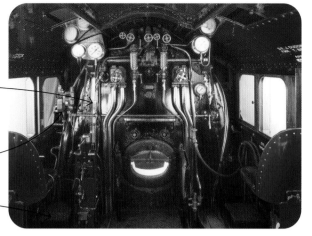

The crew consisted of a driver and a fireman. The driver controlled the locomotive with a regulator, reverser, and brake. The fireman stoked the fire to maintain a constant supply of steam, and ensured there was enough water in the boiler. He also helped the driver observe signals, especially on curves.

The regulator controls the volume of steam admitted to the cylinders, which controls the speed of the locomotive.

The brake lever operates the brake for the locomotive and the train.

The reverser allows the locomotive to be reversed.

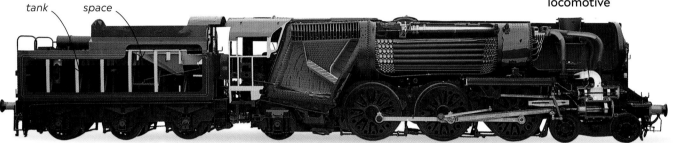

Water tank

Coal space

Front of locomotive

Coal and water are carried in a tender, behind the locomotive.

Two trailing wheels

Six driving wheels

Four leading wheels

Wheel arrangements

Steam locomotives are often described by their wheel arrangements. This locomotive has a 4–6–2 arrangement, with four leading wheels, six driving wheels, and two trailing wheels.

The steam passes through pipes into cylinders.

Chimney

Smokebox

Blast-pipe

The piston valves, sliding back and forth, admit steam to alternate sides of a piston in a power cylinder.

Section of steam locomotive

To make steam, hot gases from the firebox pass through tubes in the boiler and heat the water. The "wet" steam is collected through the regulator valve, then led to the power cylinders. Steam is admitted alternately to either side of a piston in the cylinder, pushing the piston back and forth. The piston is connected to the driving wheels through a connecting rod and crank. The "to and fro" motion of the piston turns the driving wheel. Each time the cylinder piston moves back and forth, the driving wheel completes a full rotation.

Locomotive has six coupled driving wheels, three of which are seen here

One of three power cylinders in this locomotive

Piston, linked to connecting rod

Railroads reach the world

The opening of the first "modern" railroad in England, in 1830, attracted visitors from all over the world. When other countries began to set up their own railroads, many used British designs and equipment for their locomotives, cars, and track. Later, different countries began to adapt the designs and make their own parts. By the mid-1830s, the United States was exporting steam locomotives to Europe. The railroads had a great impact on all aspects of life in many countries, from trade to travel.

Germany's first
The first steam-operated railroad in Germany opened in 1835. The English-built locomotive, seen here, was called *Der Adler*.

Headlight

Indian locomotive
This model shows a typical design of steam locomotive built in Britain for use on the East Indian Railways. Details, such as the sun blinds on the cab windows and the large headlight, were special adaptations.

Power unit

Hand rail

Hand rail

Japanese railroads
The first steam-worked rail line in Japan opened in 1872. This 19th-century woodblock contrasts transportation technology of the time—the steam locomotive—with Japan's traditional forms of transportation.

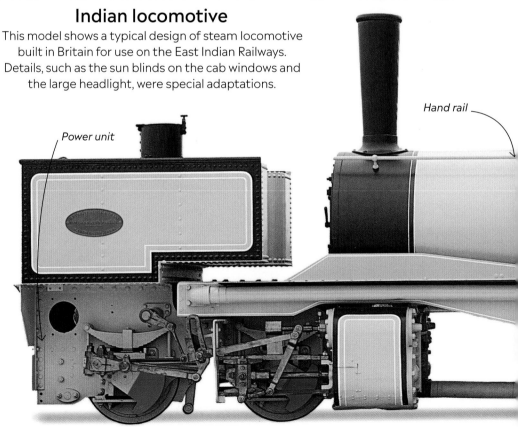

Parisian steam

This painting shows the first public steam-operated railroad in France. Opened in 1837, the line ran from Paris to Le Pecq.

Custom-built

This powerful locomotive was built in Britain in the mid-1930s for use on the Chinese National Railway. The tender is very large as it needed to carry as much water and coal as possible to operate over long distances.

Made in the USA

This is a model of a locomotive built in the US in 1843. Exported to Austria, it was designed to work on lines with steep slopes and sharp curves.

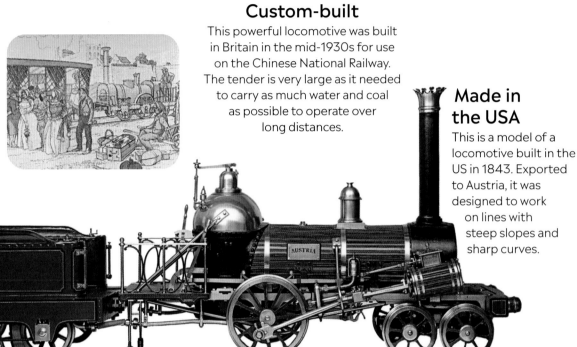

More powerful jointed locomotives (called Beyer-Garratt) of this type were later used in many other countries.

Traveling home

Built in Britain in 1909 for use in Tasmania, the first Garratt was made of jointed sections, designed for use on lines with sharp curves.

The American railroad

Railroads had a huge influence on the history and development of the US. In Europe, the new railroads served existing cities, but in the US many new towns and cities grew up as a result of the railroads. By 1869, people could cross the continent by rail. In the early 20th century, most Americans lived within 25 miles (40 km) of a railroad. Since then, the railroads have declined, largely due to competition from road and air transportation. But, there has been a renewed interest in the development of electric railroads.

The golden spike

On May 10, 1869, the United States was finally crossed by a railroad from east to west when the last spike, made of gold, joined the Union Pacific Railroad to the Central Pacific Railroad.

A tall chimney improved the draft on the fire and made the locomotive more efficient.

It's a first

The *Stourbridge Lion*, the first steam locomotive with flanged wheels to run in the US, was built in England in 1829. It was similar to the British locomotive *Agenoria* (above).

Wheel has lip, or flange

Tom Thumb

In 1830, *Tom Thumb*, a small experimental locomotive, made its first run on the Baltimore and Ohio Railroad. It also entered and lost a celebrated race with a horse-drawn train.

Driver's cab

Tender

De Witt Clinton

The first steam train in New York State was hauled by the locomotive *De Witt Clinton* in 1831. Passengers rode on top of the vehicles, as well as inside.

Building the future

The opening up of the continent by the spread of railroads was a huge achievement. The railroads played an important part in the growth, and wealth, of many towns in the US.

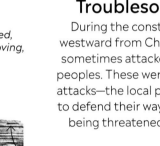

Troublesome times

During the construction of lines westward from Chicago, trains were sometimes attacked by Indigenous peoples. These were not unprovoked attacks—the local people were trying to defend their way of life, which was being threatened by developers.

Pivoted, or moving, axle

Cowcatcher kept animals from derailing the locomotive.

John Bull

This early locomotive, designed by Robert Stephenson, had a tendency to derail, and became the first locomotive to be fitted with a two-wheeled pivoted axle in front of the driving wheel.

This model is based on an 1875 locomotive that burned coal.

Typical American locomotive

This model from an 1875 design is typically American, with outside cylinders and a swiveling trolley called a "bogie" in front. The large, ornate cab helps protect the driver in bad weather. This locomotive burned coal rather than wood which, until this time, had been used almost universally in the United States.

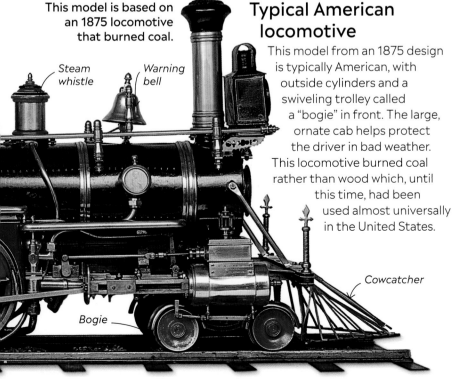

Steam whistle

Warning bell

Cowcatcher

Bogie

Cowcatcher

Unfenced tracks meant that locomotives could be derailed by animals such as buffalo. The wedge-shaped "cowcatcher" pushed the animal aside. Bells, whistles, and a large headlight also helped reduce collisions.

Building the railroads

Workman's pick

Far more work goes into building a railroad than might be expected. As trains cannot climb very steep hills, they often have to follow longer, less hilly routes. The engineer selects the route by deciding what the steepest slope can be, and considering the type of trains that will use the railroad. The route has to be kept as level as possible so builders often make cuttings or tunnels and construct bridges. Steep slopes can be avoided with "S"-shaped bends or spirals.

Blood, sweat, and tears

Early cuttings through rock, such as this 1831 example, were excavated with only basic hand tools. A large workforce was needed, and the work took many years to complete.

Hard graft

Early railroads were built with basic tools, such as this pick. Other equipment included shovels, shoulder hods (for carrying bricks), barrows, and wooden scaffolding. Gunpowder was used to blast the way through solid rock.

American construction crew, 1885

The construction crew

In the 19th century, American railroads were usually built by crews living in train cars attached to steam locomotives. The train moved the crews along the line as it was completed, as well as providing steam heating and hot water. Earth and rocks removed from cuttings were often used to build embankments.

Building bridges

Before a bridge can be built over a river, builders have to make a temporary island of rocks in the middle, or drive posts into the river bed. This early wooden arch bridge was built on wooden trestles. This design of bridge has been used extensively by the railroads.

Model of 1848 wooden arch bridge

Bridges for trains

There are different designs of railroad bridge. Cantilever bridges span long distances, for example over water. Arch bridges have a curved support on the section carrying the track. Some bridges, such as the Royal Albert Bridge (right) designed by Isambard Kingdom Brunel in 1859, are based on a mixture of designs.

Illustration of Royal Albert Bridge, near Plymouth, England

Coming and going

Passenger stations (pp. 48–49) are designed to help the arrival and departure of passengers and to provide services while they are using the station.

Who pays?

Many railroads have been financed by government-issued shares and bonds. This gold bond certificate was issued by the US government to finance railroad construction.

Channel tunnel

In 1994, the Channel Tunnel became the first ever rail link between Britain and France (pp. 62–63). The tunnel is 31 miles (49.8 km) long and took six years to build. Tunnel-boring machines worked toward one another from both sides. The machines were later buried as it was too difficult to remove them.

The arch counterbalances the point where the bridge might bend under a heavy load.

Bridges on major rivers had to be high enough so that ships could pass underneath.

Overcoming
obstacles

Sail by train

Train ferries were introduced in the mid-19th century. Train Ferry 3 (above) carried freight between Harwich and Zeebrugge from 1924 to 1945.

As railroad systems grew, engineers had to figure out how to overcome obstacles, such as valleys, mountains, lakes, and rivers. Over time, these obstacles were overcome as engineering techniques improved. Tunnels were carved through mountains, and bridges were constructed to span deep valleys and gorges. Powerful locomotives were developed that could climb up steep mountains and go around tight curves. Today, there are many high-speed trains on purpose-built lines that can travel over even the most difficult terrain.

Crossing water
The Firth of Forth bridge in Scotland was opened in 1890. It is the world's oldest railroad cantilever bridge (pp. 20–21) and is still in use today.

Tourist attraction
Mountain climbing and sightseeing by steam train was a great tourist attraction in the 1800s. The Snowdon Mountain Railway opened in Wales in 1896, using a rack and pinion system to climb the steep slopes.

Mount Washington Cog Railway
The world's first mountain rack railroad opened in 1869 in New Hampshire. This line originally used a wrought-iron rack, somewhat like a ladder.

Model of Kitson-Meyer type of tank locomotive built in 1903

A.C.N.R

Swiveling power bogie

Staying power

Powerful locomotives were needed in rugged countryside with steep slopes and tight bends. To help these long, heavy machines to go around tight curves, swiveling trolleys with wheels (bogies) were attached underneath the frame carrying the boiler.

Rigi railroad

In 1873, a steam-operated railroad opened to the top of Mount Rigi in Switzerland using a rack and pinion system. A toothed rack was laid between the rails, and a powered cog on the locomotive drove the train up the mountain.

Sydney Harbour Bridge

The Sydney Harbour Bridge is famous for its characteristic shape on the Sydney skyline. When it opened in 1932, it carried two railroad lines and two tram lines. Now it carries trains, eight road lanes, a footpath, and a cycle track.

The cantilever Forth Rail Bridge in Scotland is a **UNESCO World Heritage Site**.

23

Making tracks

Rails were used to guide loaded wagons long before the steam locomotive was invented. However, the early cast-iron rails were not strong enough to carry heavy steam locomotives. Cast-iron rails were replaced by stronger, wrought-iron rails until the 1870s, when steel tracks were introduced. Tracks are constantly being improved to carry heavier, faster trains. For a smoother ride, most main lines have continuously welded rails, instead of jointed short lengths. The distance between the rails is known as the gauge.

Track marks
The track layout at the approach to busy stations can be extremely complex. To enable trains to switch lines, special points (where trains change direction) were installed.

Laying tracks
Building early railroads required large groups of people working together to lift and position rails.

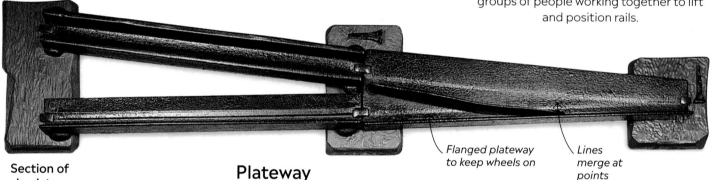

Flanged plateway to keep wheels on

Lines merge at points

Section of early plateway, 1799

Plateway
Wagons often had to be moved from one line to another. This was done by merging two lines at points, or switches. Flanged plateways (above) were replaced in the 1820s by smooth edge rails for wagons with flanged wheels (with a lip on them).

G.N.R.
80 LBS RAIL
December 1870

Bull-head rail, 1870

Saddleback or Barlow rail, used from 1849

Rail sections
Railroad engineers tried many rail designs before they came up with the flat-bottomed rail. These rail sections are some of the early designs.

"Head" of rail

L.&.Y.R.
STORES DEP.T
1884.

This type of rail has been used in Britain since the 1850s.

Flat-bottomed rail, 1884

Plate rail

Early rails, such as this plate rail from 1808, were made of cast iron in short sections, and supported by stone sleepers.

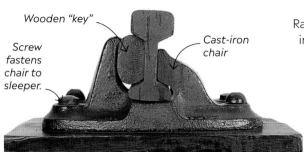

Outside flange to guide wheels without a flange

Dangerous times

Railroad dramas often featured in early films. Here the heroine is being tied to a track of flat-bottomed rails.

Wooden "key"

Screw fastens chair to sleeper.

Cast-iron chair

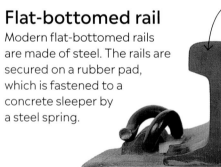

Bull-head rail

This section of steel bull-head rail is secured in a cast-iron chair by a wooden "key." The chair is secured to a wooden sleeper by large screws.

Making changes

Problems arose where railroads with different gauges met. Changing trains was particularly difficult for passengers with a lot of luggage.

Flat-bottomed rail

Modern flat-bottomed rails are made of steel. The rails are secured on a rubber pad, which is fastened to a concrete sleeper by a steel spring.

Head of steel rail

Steel spring secures rail to sleeper.

Sleeper supports the track and keeps the gauge correct.

Fish-belly rails

These cast-iron rails were designed for strength. A deeper section, halfway along the rail, was designed to resist heavy weights.

Flanged wheel fits over plain edge rail.

F. D. BANISTER Esq, C.E.

Gauge measure

Special steel rails were used to check the gauge (distance) between rails. The gauge was measured from the inside edge of one rail to the inside edge of the other. The standard gauge in Britain, and most of Europe and North America, is 4 ft 8½ in (1,435 mm).

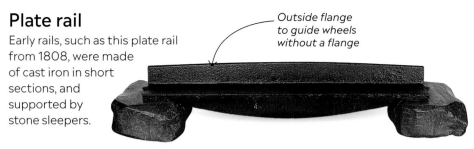

Freight trains

The earliest trains were freight trains that carried goods such as coal. At first, these trains consisted of two or three simple wagons hauled by a horse. However, with the development of the steam locomotive (pp. 10–11) trains became much longer and faster, making rail freight more efficient. In the early days, all freight trains were very slow because their basic brake systems could not stop trains fast enough in an emergency. Technical developments since then mean that freight trains can run at higher speeds.

Go by rail
This East German stamp shows how moving heavy goods by rail helps reduce road congestion.

Shedding the load
Modern freight trains carry goods in huge, standard-size containers (pp. 62–63). These can be stacked and moved from train to ship, truck, or aircraft without unpacking. Previously, cranes had to unload hundreds of different-size containers.

Caboose
Most freight trains ran with wagons that were not connected to brakes. The only means of controlling the train was to apply the brake on the locomotive and the guard's hand brake on the caboose. This meant that freight trains could travel no faster than 30 mph (50 kph).

Milk tanker
The new railroads meant that milk and fish could be delivered speedily from rural areas to the cities. By the 1930s, milk was transported in special glass-lined tankers.

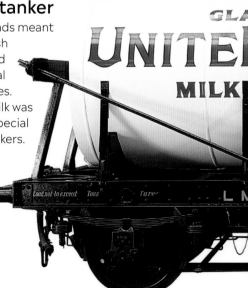

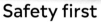

Shunter's pole with metal hook

Safety first
For many years, train cars were joined by three chain links. It was the shunter's job to couple (join) and uncouple the wagons. To avoid the risk of being injured between the wagons, shunters used a long pole with a metal hook.

Taillight
All trains carry a red taillight. This modern electric battery version gives a flashing signal.

By the mid-1950s, most freight trains in the US were hauled by diesel engines.

Bulk loads
Most freight trains now haul bulky loads in purpose-built cars, fitted with driver-operated brakes. This means that they can run safely at more than 60 mph (100 kph), like this one near Montana.

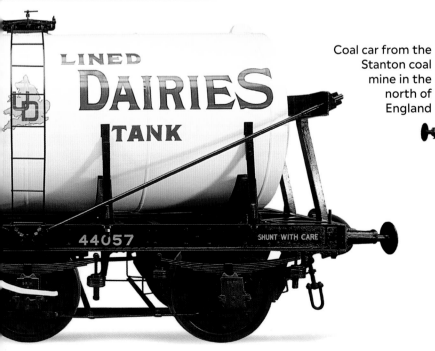

Coal car from the Stanton coal mine in the north of England

Coal car
For many years, coal was carried in Britain in simple cars owned by individual coal mines. The cars were usually loaded automatically from above, but they often had to be unloaded by workers with shovels.

American first-class ticket

Australian second-class ticket

British third-class ticket

Paying the way
These tickets are similar to the first card tickets that were made in 1837.

First, second, and third class

The first public passenger trains were very different from today's comfortable, spacious trains. They offered three different classes of accommodation. The enclosed first-class compartment had glass windows and padded seats. The second class was an open wagon with seats, while there were no seats in the third class. Over the years, trains were equipped with heating, lighting, and corridors that provided access to lavatories and to restaurant cars.

Early days
Early images of passenger trains from the 1830s show the first-class cars carrying luggage—and guards—on the roof. Second- and third-class vehicles were not enclosed.

A fresh start
The development of railroads and steamships in the 19th century led to large-scale immigration, particularly from Europe to North America. After crossing the Atlantic, immigrants traveled westward on very crowded trains.

Private rooms
First-class passengers traveled in spacious cars, and they were even able to hold private conversations.

Third-class compartment

Lavatory

WATERLOO

SMOKING

SMOKING

THIRD   6474   FIRST   LSWR

First class

First-class travelers had comfortable seats and the most legroom. Passengers in this compartment had the smoothest journey, as they were farthest from the bumps and jolts of the wheels.

Second class

Compared with first class, this compartment was simpler and had less legroom. Second-class compartments were phased out from British trains soon after this car was built.

Hard times

In the early days, third-class travel was a far cry from first class. Three or four times as many passengers were crowded into the same space.

Third class

This compartment was the simplest and had the least room. However, it was far better than the cramped conditions of the earliest third-class compartments. Located over the wheels, its occupants had a bumpy, noisy ride.

Car keys

Cars were locked when not in use. The lock is operated by a square-shaped key.

Three-in-one

This 1904 car (below) is unusual in having first-, second-, and third-class accommodation in the same vehicle, with no connecting corridor. Each compartment had access to a lavatory.

First-class compartment

Second-class compartment

Gold pass allowing senior staff free first-class travel

Traveling in style

American Pullman train pass

French free pass

By the 1850s, the railroads of Europe and the US were offering first-class passengers luxurious facilities including heating, lighting, toilets, and catering. In the US, businessman George Pullman introduced the first luxury sleeping cars in 1865, then first-class dining facilities. Soon afterward, railroad companies with long-distance passenger services started to build hotels alongside their main stations. From then on, traveling by train became a stylish affair for those who could afford it.

American free pass for Atchison, Topeka & Santa Fe railroad

China and roses

Trains with first-class dining cars would serve meals on fine china table settings. This breakfast setting was made in the 1930s and has a delicate gilt border with pink roses.

Top-notch travelers

People such as railroad directors who held free passes were able to travel first class all over the world.

Exclusive eating

Dining in a first-class restaurant car was just as enjoyable as dining in an exclusive restaurant—with the added bonus of a constantly changing view.

Travel a la mode

Striking images of elegant travelers from the 1920s and 1930s are sometimes still used by companies to promote their trains.

Anyone for cocktails?

In the 1930s, even cocktails could be ordered by first-class passengers in Britain. Each railroad company had their own monogram, which decorated glasses, silverware, and china.

30

Whodunnit?

Famous luxury trains have been the setting for many novels and films, including Agatha Christie's *Murder on the Orient Express* (1934).

Symbol of luxury

The British Pullman Company coat of arms appeared on the exterior of all its cars. Pullman cars operated in Britain from 1874 until the 1980s.

Pullman comfort

By the 1870s, American Pullman cars provided all that was needed for a long-distance journey. Travelers could even join in the Sunday hymns.

Detailed marquetry (inlay) on wood-paneled walls

Bell push for calling attendant

Pullman style

The interior of the 1914 Pullman car *Topaz* (left and below) was the ultimate in comfort. British-built Pullman cars were known for their magnificent detailed woodwork. Every armchair had a glass-topped table in front of it, together with a brass lamp and a bell push for calling the attendant. At each end of this car were private compartments for four, known as coupés.

Oval lavatory window

Brass handrails

In the signal box

The signal box plays an important role in railroad safety. In the early days, people waved flags or batons to signal when trains could move. If a train had to change direction at a junction, the "points" were operated manually to switch the train to the right track. The invention of the electric telegraph in the 1850s enabled signalmen to send an electric bell code down the line. This development led to each train being separated by a section of railroad, called a "block". The signals and points for each "block" were controlled mechanically from the signal box.

The signal box had an oil lamp in case of power failure.

On the platform

In France, the levers for signals and points were often placed behind barriers on the platform. This allowed the signalman to perform other duties between signaling trains.

Bell sounds coded message from signal boxes on either side of this one.

Yellow lever operates a distant (warning) signal.

Two red levers for stop signals pulled into "off" or "clear" position

Blue levers control locks on points, black levers control points, and white levers are spare.

What's what?

This signal box has 40 levers for operating the signals and points. Above it are electrical instruments to send and receive signals. Other instruments, called block instruments, indicate whether the line is empty, or occupied by a train. There are also "locks" between the instruments, signals, and the track. These ensure that trains are correctly signaled, and that a train cannot be overlooked if it has broken down.

Single line electric key token instrument

Staffs for a journey in the opposite direction were locked into the key token until the line was clear.

A helping hand

When signalman James Wide lost both his legs in a railroad accident in South Africa, he trained his pet baboon Jack to operate the railroad signals under supervision. From 1881 to 1890, Jack carried out his job with no errors.

Three-position block instrument

This instrument indicated to the signalman the state of the line between his box and the one before.

Bell tapper

To ask if the line was clear, the signalman used a bell tapper to send bell codes to the boxes on either side of him.

All clear

To operate the points and signals, the signalman had to pull the long levers that were linked to the points by rods, and to the signals by cables.

Three-position pegging block instrument

This instrument sent information to the three-position block instrument. It also displayed the state of the line.

Extra protection

Trains that traveled both ways on single lines depended on key token instruments. A signal could be given to the driver only once he had been handed a metal staff, coded for the journey.

Modern signal box

In the early 1900s, signal boxes were manually operated. A modern signaling control center is programmed to run automatically unless there is a problem, such as a failed train, derailment, or broken signal. Then the signaler can set alternative routes to deal with the problem.

Following the signs

The first train drivers relied on hand signals given by railroad policemen to avoid collisions with other trains. Later, mechanical signals were introduced. As train speeds rose, more sophisticated equipment was needed to improve rail safety. By the 1920s, railroads were equipped with electric color light signals that were more powerful and easier to see at a distance, especially at night. All high-speed main lines now use color light signals that, along with the points on the track, are indicated automatically in the signal box.

Stop the train!
At small rural stations in Australia, passengers stopped the train by waving a tin flag.

The red, square-ended arm is horizontal, meaning "stop."

Signalman's badge

Identification
Most people working on the railroads wore identification badges as part of their uniform.

Signaling oil lamp
In the past, the guard would signal to the driver at a station using a flag. At night, an oil lamp was used. The glass in this lamp was rotated to give a green (go), red (stop), or white (general) signal.

Three-aspect guard's lamp

Mechanical semaphore signal
The upper arm of this mechanical signal indicates whether or not a train should stop. The lower arm serves as a distant (warning) signal. It tells the driver to prepare to stop at the next signal. Here both signals are horizontal and indicate "stop."

Truncheons and armband
Early railroad policemen used different colored flags to signal that the line was clear, or that a train must stop or proceed with caution. The railroad police wore armbands for identification and carried ornate truncheons in case of trouble.

Armband and truncheons

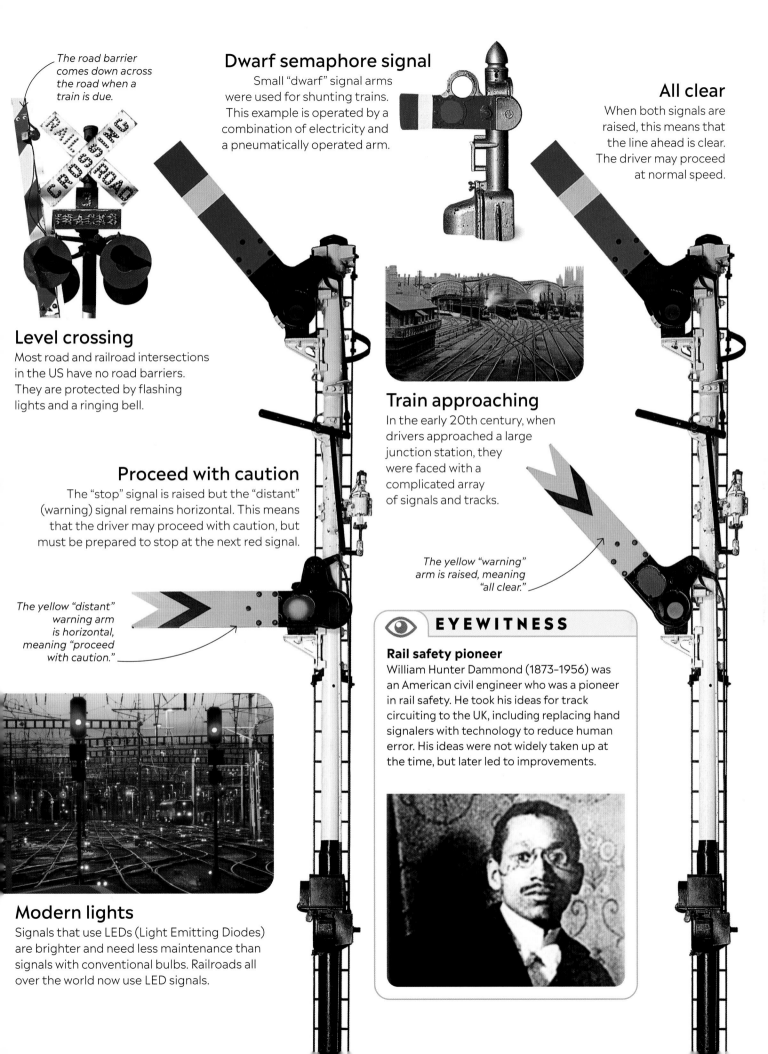

The road barrier comes down across the road when a train is due.

Dwarf semaphore signal

Small "dwarf" signal arms were used for shunting trains. This example is operated by a combination of electricity and a pneumatically operated arm.

All clear

When both signals are raised, this means that the line ahead is clear. The driver may proceed at normal speed.

Level crossing

Most road and railroad intersections in the US have no road barriers. They are protected by flashing lights and a ringing bell.

Train approaching

In the early 20th century, when drivers approached a large junction station, they were faced with a complicated array of signals and tracks.

Proceed with caution

The "stop" signal is raised but the "distant" (warning) signal remains horizontal. This means that the driver may proceed with caution, but must be prepared to stop at the next red signal.

The yellow "warning" arm is raised, meaning "all clear."

The yellow "distant" warning arm is horizontal, meaning "proceed with caution."

Modern lights

Signals that use LEDs (Light Emitting Diodes) are brighter and need less maintenance than signals with conventional bulbs. Railroads all over the world now use LED signals.

Post haste

The traveling post office was designed to handle all the jobs carried out in a normal post office—while the train sped along. Without stopping, this train car could pick up mail from specially designed equipment beside the track. The mail was then sorted and put into sacks to be dropped off along the route. The equipment for collecting and dropping off the mail was located at one end of the vehicle. The rest held sorting tables, pigeon-holes, and sacks for sorted mail.

American mail

This American locomotive from the 1870s is hauling a mail train. Mailbags are thrown down for collection, while similar bags to be picked up hang from a post.

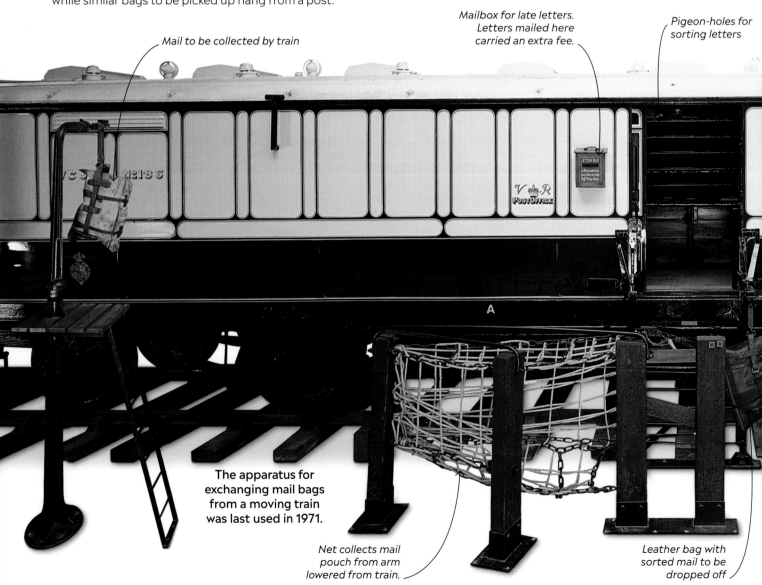

Mail to be collected by train

Mailbox for late letters. Letters mailed here carried an extra fee.

Pigeon-holes for sorting letters

The apparatus for exchanging mail bags from a moving train was last used in 1971.

Net collects mail pouch from arm lowered from train.

Leather bag with sorted mail to be dropped off

What goes where?

Incoming mail was emptied onto the sorting table, and individual letters were put into pigeon-holes. When there were enough letters for one destination, they were bundled up and put in a sack. The sacks were dropped off along the route.

Mail by rail

The strong association between trains and mail is illustrated by this 1974 Liberian postage stamp.

Swiftly by post

The "Irish Mail" ran between London and Holyhead from 1848 until 2002. As well as mail, the train also carried passengers, and offered sleeping accommodation.

Net picks up mail bag.

Traveling Post Office car, 1885

Post office on wheels

In 1838, it was decided that the Royal Mail should be carried by rail, rather than by mail coaches. In the US, the first purpose-built railroad Post Office car ran in 1864. The railroads are still used today by mail services around the world.

Picking up

This cigarette card shows a Traveling Post Office train picking up local mail at speed.

Trackside equipment

Mail to be picked up was suspended beside the track in a pouch, which was swept into a net put out from the train just before the collection point. Mail to be dropped off hung from an arm that swung out just before the train reached the collecting net.

Road to rail

This British mail van is delivering mail to a local train station. The mail was taken to a mainline station, before being put aboard a Traveling Post Office Train (TPO). The last TPO ran in Britain in 2004.

Electric trains

Engineers developed the first electric trains toward the end of the 19th century. Some locomotives collected power from overhead cables, while others took power from a third "live" rail on the track. Electric locomotives have many advantages over steam and diesel power. They are faster, quieter, and easier to run. Although building an electric railroad or electrifying an existing one is expensive, electric trains are both economical and efficient, and are now widely used on underground and commuter services around the world.

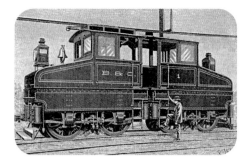

American first

The first electric locomotives on an American main line were introduced on the Baltimore and Ohio Railroad in 1895. This route passed through many tunnels, which had filled with choking fumes during the days of steam.

Early electric locomotive

This electric locomotive was built to replace steam locomotives on a freight line. The locomotive was designed to collect the electric current either by overhead pantograph or from a third "live" rail.

The pantograph, or the "arm," on top collects current from the overhead power line.

This electric locomotive was built in 1904 by the North Eastern Railway, England.

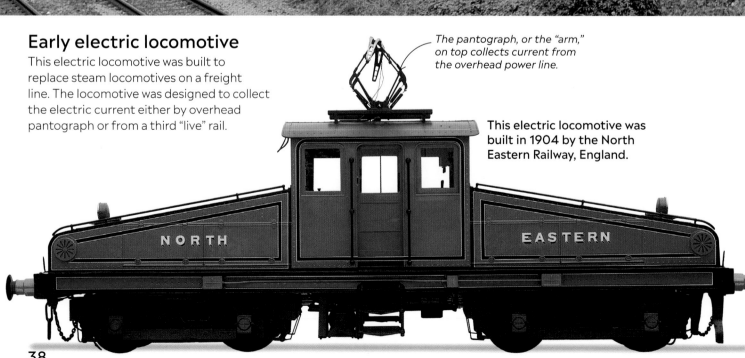

NORTH   EASTERN

Swift and safe

The French railroads used striking posters to advertise their new electric services in the early 1900s. This poster promoted the fast, clean electric trains running from Paris to Versailles.

Werner von Siemens
German engineer Werner von Siemens (1816–1892) made his name at an exhibition in Berlin, Germany, in 1879. He showcased the first practical electric passenger train. By doing so, he laid the future for the world's railroads for almost a century.

Le Mistral

This classic French train was hauled by a powerful electric locomotive. It was famed for its comfortable high-speed service between Paris and Nice.

Changing designs

The latest designs of electric trains always run the risk of being overshadowed by better, more advanced designs. The fastest electric locomotives in the UK are the Class 91, but the Hitachi 800 series trains—the Azuma—used on the electrified main line between London and Edinburgh in Scotland can accelerate and slow down much more quickly, allowing them to reduce the journey time by as much as 18 minutes.

Very, very fast

The world speed record for a passenger train was achieved by France's TGV (Train à Grande Vitesse) in 2007 when it reached 357 mph (574.8 kph). The orange TGV, introduced in 1981, was in operation until 2020. It was made up of eight cars with an electric locomotive at either end.

The first practical
electric railroad was designed by German engineer Werner von Siemens
in 1879.

Diesel power

The invention of the diesel-powered locomotive, along with the electric locomotive, signaled that the age of steam was drawing to a close. The diesel engine was first demonstrated in 1893 by German engineer Dr. Rudolph Diesel, who went on to build the world's first reliable diesel engine in 1897. In most diesel locomotives, the engine powers a generator that produces an electric current. This drives the locomotive's electric motors, which turn the wheels.

Plastic top protects from grease and dirt.

Driver's cap
Steam-engine drivers wore special caps to signify their position. The caps were also useful for keeping soot and coal dust out of the hair.

Fan cools generator

The diesel engine
In a diesel engine, heavy diesel oil is injected into a cylinder of hot air. The fuel ignites, and the energy released drives the generator. The generator makes electricity, which drives a motor that turns the wheels.

Generator produces an electric current, which is used to drive the wheels

Diesel engine drives generator

DELTIC

Snack time

Train drivers often had a snack and hot drink along the way. The lunch box and thermos here are from the days of steam.

Thermos for hot drinks

EYEWITNESS

Inventing the diesel engine

German engineer Dr. Rudolph Diesel (1858–1913) created a compression-ignition engine in 1893. By 1900, his engines were in practical use in locomotives. However, their name was too long and complex, so they became known as diesels after the inventor.

High-speed diesel

One of the first successful high-speed diesel trains was the American *Zephyr*. In 1936, it achieved an average speed of 83.3 mph (134 kph) over the 1,000-mile (1,609-km) route from Chicago to Denver.

Time saver

High-speed diesel-electric trains are designed to save time and labor. Instead of the traditional set of cars hauled by a locomotive, the cars travel between two diesel-electric power cars. At the end of the journey, the locomotive does not have to be replaced.

Trans-Europ-Express

The Trans-Europ-Express was a fast, luxurious service, designed to transport businesspeople between major European cities. The diesel-electric trains on these lines only catered for first-class passengers.

Prototype British Rail *Deltic* diesel-electric locomotive, 1955

Prototype locomotive

When this Deltic diesel-electric locomotive was built in 1955, it was the most powerful diesel-electric single-unit locomotive in the world. In 1961, the Deltics replaced the powerful steam locomotives on the East Coast main line between London and Edinburgh (pp. 46–47). In the 20 years that they worked this line, they each ran more than 3 million miles (4.8 million km).

East German stamp featuring a diesel locomotive for shunting and local freight services

Long distance by train

Early journeys on long-distance railroads were often slow and uncomfortable. Over time, the facilities on long-distance trains improved with the introduction of heating, lighting, and special cars for sleeping and dining. Today, most business people fly on longer journeys to save time. Long-distance trains, however, remain popular with tourists. For those who are not in a hurry, traveling by train is an excellent way to see a country's landscape and scenery.

Straight and narrow
The first through service from Sydney on the east coast of Australia to Perth on the west coast was introduced in 1970. The luxury *Indian Pacific* train covers the 2,704-mile- (4,352-km-) route in four days.

Containers for tea and coffee

Saucepan

Snack time
Many passengers on long-distance journeys brought their own refreshments in baskets, such as this one containing tea-making equipment. Self-catering on trains remained popular even after the introduction of restaurant cars in 1879.

Wagons-Lits car
The Wagons-Lits Company, founded in 1876, operated high-quality sleeping and dining cars across Europe.

Unification by rails
In 1891, Czar Alexander III of Russia proposed the Trans-Siberian railroad as a way to connect different parts of his country and promote economic growth. In a letter to his son, he wrote that it will "facilitate communications ... and ... secure the peaceful prosperity of this Country."

Blue Train
A luxury train has run between Cape Town and Pretoria in South Africa since 1903. In 1939, the *Blue Train* was introduced on this 956-mile (1,540-km) stretch, and it is now regarded as one of the most luxurious trains in the world.

Sleeping car

Passengers could travel in comfortable sleeping cars from the 1860s in the United States, and from the 1870s in Europe. This two-berth compartment on a 1936 Wagons-Lits sleeping car traveled overnight between London, Paris, and Brussels. During the day, the lower berth was converted into seats. Trains on this route crossed the Channel on board a train ferry.

Train ferry

The Dover–Dunkerque train ferry, linking England with France, came into service in 1936. The ferry ceased running in 1995 and all freight traffic now goes by truck or via the Channel Tunnel.

Trans-Siberian railroad

A passenger train between Moscow and Vladivostok makes one of the longest regular train journeys in the world. It takes eight days to travel 5,778 miles (9,297 km).

Super service

The American *Super Chief* service ran between Los Angeles and Chicago. Known for its fine dining, it established a reputation as the best long-distance train in the United States.

Super Chief ticket of 1938

Royal coat
of arms on
Gladstone

Royal trains

Some of the most splendid train cars ever built were constructed for the British Royal Family. Since the first royal train journey in 1839, the Royal Family have traveled by train when making longer trips around Britain. The railroads offered greater comfort, space, and privacy than road transportation. When built, the royal carriages represented the latest in design and technology. Royal trains are still used today.

Royal regalia

Locomotives that were used to haul royal trains, like *Gladstone* (above and below), usually carried elaborate cast-metal coats of arms and flags.

Gladstone's lamp

Oil headlights on royal locomotives were often decorated, such as this one from *Gladstone*.

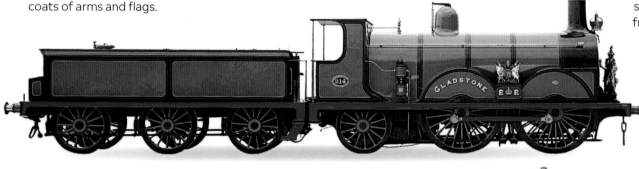

Attendants' compartment

Royal stations

Some stations were built especially for royal use, such as this one at Gosport, which Queen Victoria used when traveling to her residence on the Isle of Wight. The station was richly decorated for her arrival.

By day, the Queen sat in the coupé compartment, which had end windows.

N°. 2

Queen's carriage

The first royal saloon was made for the Dowager Queen Adelaide in 1842 (right). The design was based on three stagecoach compartments, with a beautifully furnished and upholstered interior. It is thought that the Queen traveled during the day in the end (or coupé) compartment, with close attendants in the middle compartment.

The footrail and the step above allowed access from ground level.

Queen Victoria's day saloon

No expense was spared in the decoration of the day saloon, which was chosen by Queen Victoria. The wood was maple, the upholstery was blue watered silk, and the ceilings were covered in white quilted silk. The saloon was originally lit with oil lamps, but in 1895 newly developed electric lighting and bells for calling attendants were added.

Stretching out

At night, the Queen would transfer to the compartment at the other end, where the cushions were rearranged into a bed. The boxlike extension at the end provided extra room for feet and legs.

Sleeping compartment

"Boot," or boxlike, extension

Wooden chassis (framework) with four wheels

Queen Victoria's lavatory

This toilet and washing compartment was beautifully furnished in maple and blue silk.

King Edward VII's smoking compartment

The King's wood-paneled compartment of 1902 contained fans, heaters, and even cigar-lighters.

Queen Alexandra's bedroom

The Queen could use the buttons above her bed to summon her servants during the night.

Queen Mary's day compartment

The saloon contained a day compartment, together with a dressing room, bathroom, and bedroom.

Record breakers

From the earliest days of steam to the present day, speed records have been, and are still being, set and broken. For Britain and the US, breaking the speed barrier of one hundred miles per hour was a special target. This target was supposedly met in 1893, when an American locomotive was claimed to have reached a speed of 112½ mph (181 kph), and in 1904, when a British locomotive was timed at 102 mph (164 kph). However, serious doubts were later cast on both these claims.

Fast movers

The first steam engines designed to run at 100 mph (161 kph) on every trip operated the 1935 *Hiawatha* service between Chicago and Minneapolis/St. Paul. The service holds the record for the fastest steam-powered run between two stations on a scheduled service.

The best ever

The brass plaque on the boiler of *Mallard* commemorates the world speed record for a steam locomotive set on July 3, 1938.

Steam train of the *Hiawatha* service

Like a bullet

When opened in 1964, the Japanese electric Shinkansen, or "bullet train," between Tokyo and Osaka was the first of a new generation of high-speed railroads built exclusively for intercity passenger trains.

The Journey Shrinker

In 1985, the British Rail High Speed Train (HST) reached a record speed for a diesel locomotive of 144 mph (232 kph), earning it the name "The Journey Shrinker."

The fastest ever

The TGV (*Train à Grande Vitesse*), a French electric high-speed train, was introduced in 1981 between Paris and Lyon. TGVs run on specially designed tracks, and travel up to 200 mph (320 kph). In 2007, a modified TGV achieved a world record of 357 mph (574.8 kph) on the Paris to Strasbourg line.

Steam record

The steam locomotive *Mallard* was designed by British engineer Sir Nigel Gresley. In July 1938, *Mallard* set a world speed record for a steam locomotive of 126 mph (203 kph). It was pulling a special train on the main line between London and Edinburgh. This record still stands.

Mallard was built by the London North Eastern Railway in 1938.

At the station

The very first stations were simple wooden shelters built next to the rail track. Today, some small rural stations are still very simple buildings, providing little more than a ticket counter and a waiting room. But in many major towns and cities, train stations are busy transportation hubs, offering a wide range of shops, cafes, restaurants, and parking lots. Often, the station is one of the largest buildings in town, with imposing architecture in styles from all ages from classical to ultra-modern.

A large clock is often the focal point of a station.

Country station

Simple stations in rural areas often had a very low platform, or none at all. Passengers entered or left the train by climbing onto steps on the train cars.

Time in hand

To keep trains to a strict timetable, stations had large clocks, while railroad staff carried pocket watches.

Late 19th-century pocket watch

Handbell

Before electricity was available to operate electric bells, handbells were rung to announce the arrival of a train.

London, Chatham, and Dover Railway insignia

Railroad time

In the early days, trains that ran east to west in large countries such as the US experienced problems with timekeeping. Eventually, these countries were divided into different time zones, so the time changed whenever a train crossed into a new zone.

Waterloo station

Large stations, such as this one, are designed so that huge numbers of passengers can quickly board or leave their train during peak hours.

Tickets please!

Tickets were proof that passengers had paid the fare. A ticket inspector marked the ticket with a clipper so that it could not be used again. Modern digital tickets usually have a QR code or bar code that can be scanned at the station or on the train.

Japanese train tickets

QR code

An electronic train ticket

A first-class ticket to Basra in Iraq

Clipper

Special delivery

In the 1920s and 1930s, the railroads ferried freight to and from stations using their own road vehicles. Bicycles were used for delivering small, local parcels.

SOUTHERN RAILWAY PARCEL DELIVERY SERVICE FROM HORSTED KEYNES STATION

H.B.K

Simple metal whistle

Whistle stop

Simple whistles made from wood or metal were used by platform staff to let the driver know when a train was ready to depart.

Railroad uniform button forms part of this whistle.

Landmark station

With their imposing architecture, stations such as the Gare de Lyon in Paris became familiar landmarks.

The romance of steam

The days of steam are often portrayed as a romantic age. The classic film *Brief Encounter* (1945) is based on a chance meeting at a train station shortly after World War II.

Grand Central Station

New York's Grand Central Station is the largest train station in the world. Information boards in its huge concourse show where and when the trains are arriving and departing.

Running the railroad

British porter's cap badge

Russian railroad worker's badge

Many people are required for the smooth running of a railroad. The commercial departments specify the type, frequency, and speed of trains needed. The operating department meets these demands. The technical engineering department provides the equipment, while the civil engineering team ensures that the track and structures are functional. All this work is supported by many other departments.

Oiling the wheels
Steam train drivers were responsible for checking that their trains were in working order.

Chinese railroad worker's badge

Great Western Railway fireman's helmet

Smooth operation
Because railroad companies needed a wide variety of workers to run smoothly, they were traditionally among the world's largest employers.

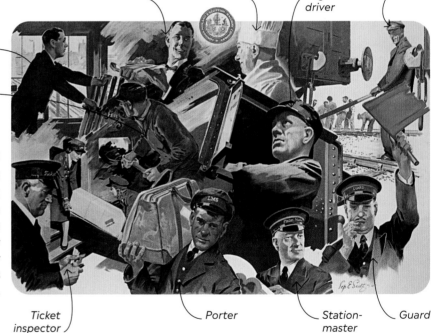

Signalman · Fireman · Waiter · Chef · Engine driver · Shunter · Ticket inspector · Porter · Station-master · Guard

Safety first
The railroads ran their own fire department, trained to deal with any special hazards. The service had its own equipment and uniform.

Travelers' helper
In the past, railroad companies owned many of the station hotels. The hotel porter assisted passengers entering and leaving the hotel.

Stationmaster
The stationmaster was in charge of all aspects of running the station and ensured that trains arrived and departed promptly.

The permanent way

A great deal of organization went into maintaining the track. The lookout man, in charge of the working team, would blow a horn to warn of an approaching train.

The railroad track was known as "the permanent way."

Indispensable

Even with today's new equipment, the signal engineer still plays a vital role. However, all modern signal equipment is designed to be "fail-safe" by showing red stop signals in case of malfunction.

The hose is fitted into the dining car's water tank.

When the wheel turns, it pumps water through the hose.

Topping up

While at the station, a long-distance train had to be stocked up with enough food and water to last until the next refueling stop. This water carrier was used to top up the dining car's tank with drinking water. The tanks for the lavatories were refilled with hoses attached to local water supplies.

Oilcan from around 1890

Useful tool

This oilcan was used for filling oil lamps. The broad base makes it difficult to knock over.

The water carrier is wheeled along the platform.

Thick, multi-stranded wick

Lighting up

Flare lamps provided light before electric battery lamps came along. The oil in the lamp was burned at the end of the wick. The lamp warned of hazards in yards, as well as being used for inspecting steam locomotives.

Oil flare lamp from around 1900

Still in steam

In most parts of the world, steam locomotives are a thing of the past. Cleaner, more efficient diesel and electric trains have taken their place. However, there is still considerable interest in steam engines among rail enthusiasts. Some modern, more efficient, steam locomotives are still used on tourist lines in countries such as Switzerland. Hundreds of preserved steam locomotives are owned by railroad societies and transportation museums around the world, and many have been carefully restored. They are used to pull trains on preserved lines, or on the quieter scenic lines of national railroad networks.

New locomotives
Completed in 2008, *Tornado* was the first main line steam locomotive to be made in the UK since 1960. It has run all over the UK in the years since and reached a milestone speed of 100 mph (161 kph) in 2017.

Keeping on track
Steam trains were used in India until the end of the 20th century. Narrow gauge locomotives, such as this one, were imported to India from France, Germany, and Japan.

In 1958, British Railways had
16,000 steam locomotives,
but by the end of 1968, there were none.

Star exhibit
Evening Star was the last steam locomotive built for British Rail in 1960. It was originally intended for freight work, but it also pulled passenger and express trains until 1966. It is now displayed in Britain's National Railway Museum.

Tourist attractions

Many steam railroads are now tourist attractions. The first was the Talyllyn Railway in Wales, saved in 1951 and run by volunteers in their spare time. Across the world, new steam locomotives have been built to reproduce old designs or to operate specifically on tourist railroads.

The building of new steam locomotives in China only ceased at the end of the 1980s.

Long live steam

In 1990, there were 7,000 steam, 4,700 diesel, and 1,200 electric locomotives in China. Steam trains were finally withdrawn from use in China in 2003.

Preserved locomotive of Fort Worth & Western Railroad

Preserved steam

The United States was quick to turn from steam power to electric and diesel power. There are, however, a large number of steam locomotives restored to working order in the US. Train enthusiasts can ride on some of the classic routes, or visit private steam centers.

Veteran locomotives

Although India and Pakistan no longer use steam locomotives, there are still a few tourist steam trains in operation. Locomotives, such as this old British tank engine, attract enthusiasts from all over the world.

All decked out

Elaborate decoration took hold in the 19th century. Striking displays promoted the services offered by railroad companies, and colorful signs were placed on tunnel entrances to reassure people unfamiliar with rail travel. As competition grew between railroad companies, decorations bearing the name of each company appeared on railroad property. Huge, colorful, cast-iron plaques were hung on railroad bridges, and company initials could even be found on the heads of copper nails for slate tiles.

Coat of arms
This Midland Railway coat of arms featured a winged monster and emblems of the cities served by the railroad.

TGV nameplate
Many of the French TGV trains' power car units are named after cities served by these trains.

Express train headboard
The headboard displayed the name of the train. It was fastened to the chimney of the locomotive that pulled the train.

Works plate
The works plate carries a locomotive's number and date, and often the name and the location of the building company. This plate also bears the name of the company's president.

American works plate

Lion crest
This crest was displayed on British Railways locomotives and carriages during the 1950s.

Southern Railway nameplate

Unique trains
Locomotives pulling special trains often carried badges created just for the occasion.

Famous names
The names given to locomotives ranged from classical and famous figures to railroad directors and names of places served by the railroad.

DOMINION OF NEW ZEALAND

London and North Eastern Railway nameplate

Brass nameplate
This brass nameplate commemorated links with the British Commonwealth.

Knight of the Golden Fleece
This classical name was carried by an express locomotive of the Great Western Railway.

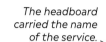

The crown indicates that the railroad was the only one in Canada operated with a Royal Charter.

KNIGHT OF·THE GOLDEN FLEECE

The headboard carried the name of the service.

DOMINION ATLANTIC **39** RAILWAY.

ATLANTIC COAST EXPRESS

Gold Coast Railway
The coat of arms of the Gold Coast Railway featured an elephant, a familiar sight in the country now known as Ghana.

Number plate
This brass number plate is from a 1902 locomotive belonging to the Canadian Dominion Atlantic Railway.

What goes where?
The headboard and nameplate were carried on the locomotive. The railroad company's coat of arms was displayed on the locomotive and on the carriages.

Good publicity
Locomotives were usually named after towns and cities served by the railroad, as seen on this nameplate of the London Midland and Scottish Railway.

CITY OF MANCHESTER

Local wildlife
A black swan was the symbol of the Western Australian Government Railways from 1890 to 1976.

Scottish flag

English flag

The Caledonian
The shields on this headboard carry motifs of the English and Scottish flags.

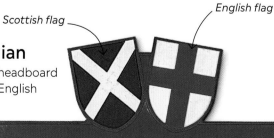

THE CALEDONIAN

WESTERN AUSTRALIAN GOVERNMENT RAILWAYS

Traveling underground

The success of the railroads in bringing people to large cities also caused problems such as road congestion. In London, UK, this led to the world's first underground rail system in 1863, built by digging a trench and then covering it to form a tunnel. Despite the smoky atmosphere, it was quicker and easier than road travel. Later, deeper tunnels were built, and electric trains, elevators, and escalators were introduced. The system became known as the "tube." Over time, other cities around the world began to develop their own electric underground railroads.

Luxury for all

The first underground rail in Moscow opened in 1933. Its stations were famed for their luxurious decor.

All packed in

Underground cars have automatic sliding doors and wide gangways to provide as much space as possible for commuters, both seated and standing.

Early days

Early paintings of the first underground railroad show wide tunnels, with natural light filtering through. In reality, the smoke and fumes made traveling on the underground dirty and unpleasant.

Metropolitan Railway Tank Locomotive

This classic underground steam locomotive was built for the Metropolitan Railway in London in 1866. To reduce smoke and steam in the tunnels, the locomotive was fitted with a valve to divert smoke and steam into its water tanks. Unfortunately, this slowed it down. To make up time, drivers did not always operate the valve in the tunnels. Conditions could become unpleasant, especially during rush hours.

The train driver stood here.

Water tank

METROPOLITAN 23 RAILWAY.

The Metro Man
Indian engineer E. Sreedharan oversaw the construction and initial operation of the Delhi Metro for 16 years from 1995 until his retirement in 2011. This was a very challenging undertaking, but he simply said "I refused to give in" and successfully completed the project.

Uniform badge
Railroad staff were easily recognized by the striking badges worn as part of their uniform.

London Transport badge with heraldic griffins, from early 1930s

Paris Metro
The underground railroad opened in Paris in 1900, and was called the *Metro*. *Metro* stations are very close together and easily recognizable by their signs. Any point in the city center is within comfortable walking distance of a station.

Reading the map
The Paris *Metro* map relates the route of the train lines to the streets above them. This London Underground map of 1927 is roughly based on a geographical map of London. Maps used today make no attempt to do this, and are not to scale.

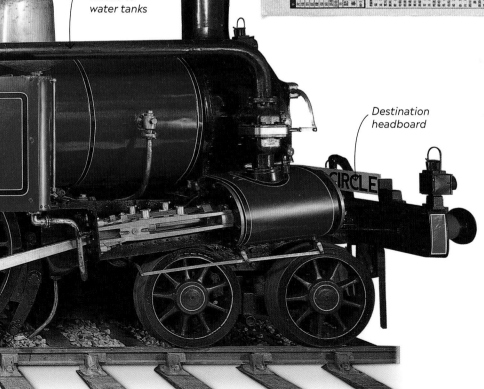

Pipe leading steam and smoke to water tanks

Destination headboard

Where are we?
Japan's underground railroad, which opened in Tokyo in 1927, is extremely large and busy. This Tokyo subway ticket has a route map on one side.

Automated trains
Most modern rapid transit systems, such as the Metro in Washington, D.C., (above), are ideal for automation. Over the past few years, several countries, including India and France, have introduced driverless trains on their underground rail networks.

Up in the air

Some railroads hang under rails affixed to overhead structures. These can be of two types: suspended, where the train hangs under a rail or rails, and "straddle," where the train fits over a single rail. Suspended trains have wheels that fit onto the rails, so there is no risk of trains falling to the ground. Overhead systems with a single rail are called monorails. Modern overhead railroads are cheaper to build, offer a good view, and avoid conflict with road traffic. However, they are often noisier than street trains due to their elevated position.

New York's elevated railroad

As street congestion in cities grew, elevated railroads were seen as a cheaper and more flexible alternative to underground railroads. This elevated railroad was built in New York in the 1880s.

Montmartre funicular

Funiculars are a type of cable railroad, used to carry freight up and down slopes. They were originally built with a double track to balance the system so that loaded cars traveling down one line helped pull up empty cars on the other line. Most funiculars are now electric and carry passengers. This funicular in Montmartre, Paris, was built in 1900, and still operates today.

Out of the way

Monorails, such as this one at the National Motor Museum in England, are often used to transport visitors around exhibitions. Because they are elevated, these railroads can cover ground crowded with pedestrians without causing any obstruction.

The first monorail

The first commercial monorail opened in Wuppertal, Germany, in 1901 and is still operational today. For much of its 8-mile (12.9-km) journey, the railroad straddles the Wupper River.

Giant, steel legs support the monorail track.

428

👁 **EYEWITNESS**

Eugen Langen
German engineer Eugen Langen (1833–1895) developed an overhead electric railroad system that included "one-rail" in the title. This led to the use of the word "monorail" for this type of railroad. His system was chosen for the city of Wuppertal.

Novelty value

Monorails have great novelty value and are often seen in theme parks. This open-car monorail operates in a Dutch zoo, where animals may be viewed and photographed in complete safety.

Monorail exhibited in Brisbane, Australia, at the Expo '88 fair

ERECTED OVER L·N·E·R LINE— MILNGAVIE STATION (NEAR GLASGOW)

G·B·R

Glasgow rail plane

This rail plane was developed in the 1920s by George Bennie and tried out near Glasgow in Scotland. It was a suspended monorail that traveled along the track using a propeller similar to those used on airplanes. However, despite interest from around the world, the rail plane did not progress beyond the experimental stage.

IBERIA

Train with one rail

In most modern monorails, the train straddles the supporting structure. It is balanced and guided by side panels that contain guide wheels. The train runs on electric power, collected from conductor strips set in the side webs of the rail.

Caboose   Milk car   Tanker car   Cement car

Trains **for fun**

No sooner had railroads been invented for transportation than people began to build them for fun. These ranged from simple toy trains for children to complex scale models of full-size trains. The earliest toy trains, made of flat pieces of lead, were followed by wooden trains with rotating wheels. These wooden models were replaced by tin-plate trains running on model tracks, driven at first by clockwork and later by electricity. Over time, enthusiasts began to make and collect miniature scale models of full-size trains.

Smaller than life
Miniature railroads are built just for entertainment. They have been popular since the 19th century, especially when pulled by steam.

These images are cut out and made into three-dimensional locomotives.

Cut and paste
Miniature cardboard cutout models are an alternative and cheaper way of collecting models of famous locomotives.

Grand junction locomotive
This model of a classic freight locomotive dates from 1846. It has all the features of a full-size train in working order—such as oil lamps, levers, and whistles.

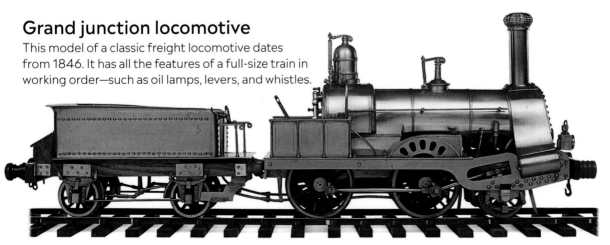

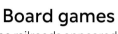

1930s freight train set

Tin-plate trains

British tin-plate clockwork train sets were well-made and built to last. Such sets included lengths of track and other accessories, such as points and tunnels.

Thomas the Tank Engine

Paintings and photographs of railroad scenes are often used for jigsaw puzzles. This puzzle features Thomas the Tank Engine, the main character in a popular series of 1940s children's books and a more recent television show.

Board games

The railroads appeared in many aspects of everyday life. They even featured in family games, such as this French board game of the 1870s.

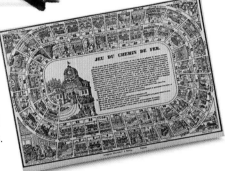

Precision-made model

Models are often made of famous locomotives, such as this detailed model of a heavy freight steam locomotive built in the early 1940s for America's Union Pacific Railroad.

Scaled to size

Accurate working scale models are usually made as a hobby by skilled craftspeople. This model, *Lady of Lynn*, is of an express locomotive that ran on the Great Western Railway in Britain in 1908.

The perfect present

Whether simple toys or miniature models, trains still fascinate children and adults alike. Train sets have always made ideal gifts for children. A basic train set can be built up to include stations, bridges, tunnels, signals, and all the elements of a modern railroad.

The Docklands Light Railway is elevated above street level.

Driverless trains

Light rail transit systems, such as the Docklands Light Railway in London, UK (above), provide a regular service in congested city centers. The driverless electric trains are controlled by a central computer system.

Into the future

New trains and track are constantly being developed, using new materials and more environmentally friendly power sources such as hydrogen. In some cities, electric rapid transit systems have been built using driverless trains that run on rubber tires along a concrete track. Some countries have developed faster trains to run on existing lines. New lines are also being built. Because they produce less pollution than road traffic, and can carry larger cargoes, trains are believed to be the best form of transportation for the future.

Freight trains carry anything from cars to fuel or sheep.

A freight train removes on average 76 semis and trucks from the roads.

Magnetic levitation

Maglev is short for magnetic levitation. Instead of traveling on wheels on a rail, the train hovers up to ½ in (15 mm) above a metal track, and is pulled along by magnets. This system's many advantages include having no moving parts to wear out, little maintenance, and very quiet trains.

Shanghai Maglev at the Shanghai Pudong International Airport, China

Taking the bend

Tilting trains developed by the Italian Railways are designed to run high-speed services on upgraded traditional lines. When a curve is detected by the sensor controls, the train is tilted by a hydraulic mechanism to ensure passenger comfort as it goes through the curve.

Pendolino train tilting as it rounds a bend on the West Coast Main Line in the UK.

Tried and failed

The first gas turbine locomotive was built for Swiss Railways in 1941. This picture shows a Canadian National Railway gas turbine-powered train. Like many trains of its kind, it proved to be unreliable, and was withdrawn from service in the 1980s.

Double decker

This double-stack container train is carrying freight on the Cajon Pass in California. Double-stack container trains carry much more freight than conventional trains, saving fuel costs as well as the cost of building new tracks.

Two freight containers sit on top of each other.

Super train

When the Channel Tunnel opened in 1994, trains ran from Waterloo, London, UK. In 2007, a new terminus opened at London St. Pancras International. Eurostar electric train services currently run from London to Paris, France, in 2 hours 15 minutes and from London to Brussels, Belgium, in under two hours.

Green trains

The climate crisis has seen train builders seek new forms of power to drive rolling stock and find an alternative to diesel for heavy freight. In 2019, the UK launched its first hydrogen-powered train HydroFlex in an effort toward reducing carbon emissions.

Great train journeys

There are more than 800,000 miles (1.3 million km) of track on Earth, and each year people travel over 1,367 billion miles (2,200 billion km) by rail, riding everything from Japan's bullet trains to Africa's luxurious *Blue Train*. For extreme tastes, there's the world's steepest rail climb up Ecuador's Devil's Nose Mountain.

The Canadian (Canada)

Traveling 2,775 miles (4,466 km) from Vancouver to Toronto, it passes through the wilderness of the Rockies, the great plains, and the Ontario lake lands.

California *Zephyr* (US)

Running from San Francisco to Chicago, the California *Zephyr*'s 2,438-mile (3,924-km) route offers dramatic views of the Sierra Nevada Mountains and the upper Colorado River Valley.

Copper Canyon Railway (Mexico)

This 390-mile (650-km) route runs from Los Mochis, near the Pacific coast, to Chihuahua, taking in breathtaking terrain.

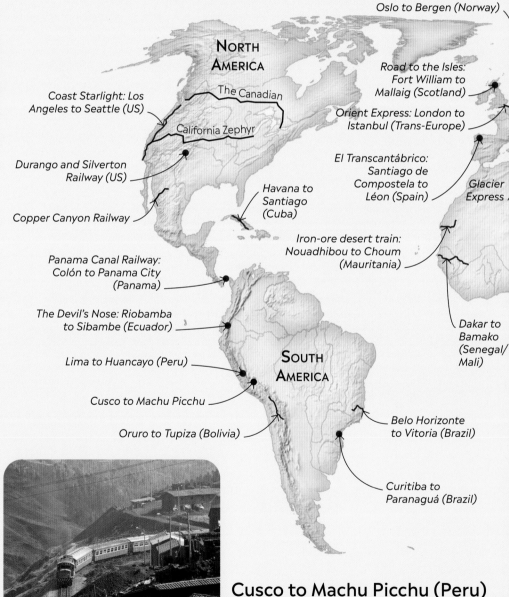

NORTH AMERICA

The Canadian

California Zephyr

Coast Starlight: Los Angeles to Seattle (US)

Durango and Silverton Railway (US)

Copper Canyon Railway

Havana to Santiago (Cuba)

Panama Canal Railway: Colón to Panama City (Panama)

The Devil's Nose: Riobamba to Sibambe (Ecuador)

Lima to Huancayo (Peru)

Cusco to Machu Picchu

Oruro to Tupiza (Bolivia)

SOUTH AMERICA

Belo Horizonte to Vitoria (Brazil)

Curitiba to Paranaguá (Brazil)

Oslo to Bergen (Norway)

Road to the Isles: Fort William to Mallaig (Scotland)

Orient Express: London to Istanbul (Trans-Europe)

El Transcantábrico: Santiago de Compostela to Léon (Spain)

Glacier Express

Iron-ore desert train: Nouadhibou to Choum (Mauritania)

Dakar to Bamako (Senegal/Mali)

Cusco to Machu Picchu (Peru)

This 70-mile (112-km) ride to Machu Picchu's ancient Inca ruins offers awe-inspiring views of the dramatic canyon along the Urubamba River.

Glacier Express (Switzerland)

Reputed to be the world's slowest express, this train travels 180 miles (291km) from Zermatt to St. Moritz, negotiating 291 bridges and 91 tunnels on the way.

Trans-Siberian Railway (Russia)

Traveling some 5,771 miles (9,288 km) through seven time zones, this is the world's longest rail journey. It runs from Moscow in the west to Vladivostok in the east.

Qingzang Railway (China)

This 1,215-mile (1,956-km) route from Lhasa, Tibet, to Xining, Qinghai Province, includes the world's highest section of track through the Tanggula Pass at 16,640 ft (5,072 m).

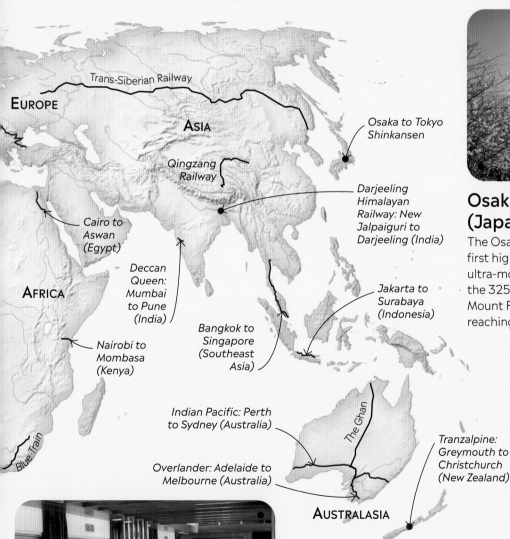

Trans-Siberian Railway

EUROPE

ASIA

Osaka to Tokyo Shinkansen

Qingzang Railway

Darjeeling Himalayan Railway: New Jalpaiguri to Darjeeling (India)

Cairo to Aswan (Egypt)

Deccan Queen: Mumbai to Pune (India)

AFRICA

Jakarta to Surabaya (Indonesia)

Nairobi to Mombasa (Kenya)

Bangkok to Singapore (Southeast Asia)

Indian Pacific: Perth to Sydney (Australia)

The Ghan

Tranzalpine: Greymouth to Christchurch (New Zealand)

Overlander: Adelaide to Melbourne (Australia)

Blue Train

AUSTRALASIA

Osaka to Tokyo Shinkansen (Japan)

The Osaka–Tokyo Shinkansen was the world's first high-speed train service. Today, the new, ultra-modern Nozomi bullet trains complete the 325-mile (525-km) route, which passes Mount Fuji, in just two-and-a-half hours, reaching speeds of around 185 mph (300 kph).

The Ghan (Australia)

The name refers to the Afghan camel trains that once trekked the same route. It takes 48 hours to travel 1,850 miles (2,979 km) from Darwin to Adelaide.

Blue Train (South Africa)

Running 994 miles (1,600 km) from Cape Town to Pretoria, this luxurious ride offers a butler service and full-size bathtubs.

Train timeline

Around 200 years ago, railroads began to revolutionize our world, opening up new opportunities for travel and trade. This new means of transportation could carry people and goods faster and farther than ever before. This timeline lists some important "firsts" in the history of trains and railroads.

1604 A track-way carrying horse-drawn coal wagons on wooden rails is built near Nottingham, UK.

1767 The world's first iron rails for coal wagons are made at Coalbrookedale Iron Works, in Shropshire, UK.

1769 In Paris, France, Nicolas Cugnot builds and demonstrates a steam-powered road carriage—the first-ever self-propelled vehicle.

Flywheel to even out the power

Trevithick's locomotive, 1804

1804 English engineer Richard Trevithick builds the world's first steam locomotive.

1812 The coal-carrying Middleton Railway in Leeds, UK, is the first commercial railroad to successfully use steam locomotives.

1825 The Stockton and Darlington Railway in County Durham, UK, is the first public steam railroad.

1828 The United States' Delaware & Hudson Railroad is the first operational railroad in North America.

1829 George and Robert Stephenson's *Rocket* wins the Rainhill Trials near Liverpool, UK.

1830 The UK's Liverpool & Manchester Railway runs the first scheduled steam passenger services.

1830 *The Best Friend of Charleston* is the first all-American-built locomotive.

1843 The steamship *Great Britain* combines with the express trains of the Great Western Railway to link London, UK, with New York City.

1853 The first railroad in India begins operating, connecting the cities of Bombay (now Mumbai) and Thane.

1854 Australia's first railroad links Port Melbourne with Melbourne, New South Wales.

1856 In the southeastern US, a railroad bridge is built over the Mississippi River for the first time.

The Golden Spike Ceremony at the opening of the US Transcontinental Railroad, 1869

1860 The *Flying Scotsman* begins running between London and Edinburgh, UK.

1863 The world's first underground railroad opens in London, UK. It is steam-powered.

1863 The first railroad is built in New Zealand.

1869 The Transcontinental Railroad spans North America from east to west.

1871 New York's Grand Central Station opens. It is the world's largest train station.

1881 The world's first public electric railroad opens in Germany.

1885 The Canadian Pacific Railroad begins operating.

1890 An electric underground railroad opens in London, UK—it is the first of its kind in the world.

1893 The world's first electric overhead railroad opens in Liverpool, UK.

1895 The Baltimore & Ohio Railroad in the United States is the first main line railroad to be electrified in the world.

1904 The Trans-Siberian Railway opens from Moscow to Vladivostok, Russia.

1904 The New York City Subway opens.

1913 The world's first regular diesel-train service begins in Sweden.

1928 The UK's *Flying Scotsman* service runs nonstop between London and Edinburgh, covering the 393-mile (632-km) route in 8 hours 3 minutes.

1932 Germany's diesel-powered "Flying Hamburger," the first purpose-built high-speed train, begins running between Hamburg and Berlin.

1932 The LMS railroad's new shunting locomotives are the first diesels on the UK rail network.

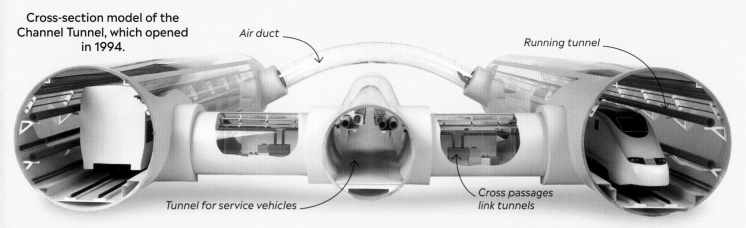

Cross-section model of the Channel Tunnel, which opened in 1994.

Air duct

Running tunnel

Tunnel for service vehicles

Cross passages link tunnels

1934 Streamlined diesel trains begin running between Los Angeles and New York City.

1934 French railroad ETAT introduces a 99-mph (159-kph), lightweight, streamlined gasoline rail car.

1935 The *Hiawatha* connecting Chicago with Minneapolis/St. Paul is the fastest scheduled steam service in the world.

1935 A world speed record for non-streamlined steam locomotives of 108 mph (173 kph) is set by the UK's LNER A3 locomotive *Papyrus*.

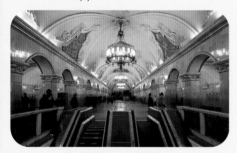

Moscow subway

1935 The Moscow subway opens its first line.

1938 In the UK, the locomotive *Mallard* sets a world record for steam traction of 126 mph (203 kph).

1941 The United States' Union Pacific Railroad unveils its new locomotive, the 4-8-8-4 Big Boy. It is the largest steam locomotive ever built.

1945 The New York Central Railroad reduces the journey time for the 928-mile (1,493-km) New York–Chicago trip to 16 hours.

1960 Container trains begin operating in the United States.

1964 Japan opens the world's first purpose-built high-speed passenger railroad—the bullet train. The line speed is 130 mph (210 kph).

1968 Steam power ends on the UK rail network.

1969 Australia opens the east–west transcontinental rail route from Sydney to Perth.

1970 In America, Penn Central Railway goes bankrupt—the largest corporate failure in US history.

1971 The US government forms AMTRAK to operate all passenger rail services in the United States.

1981 France opens its first TGV high-speed line between Paris and Lyon. It has a top speed of 186 mph (300 kph).

1984 The first double-stack container trains begin operating in the US.

1984 The world's first maglev train opens at Birmingham International Airport in the UK.

1985 British Rail's High-Speed Train sets a new record for diesel traction of 147 mph (238 kph).

1991 Germany opens its first ICE high-speed rail line.

1994 The Channel Tunnel opens, providing an undersea rail link between the UK and France.

2001 In Australia, the world's longest ever train measures 4½ miles (7.3 km). It consists of 682 cars and eight locomotives.

Japan's N700 bullet train, 2007

2003 Japan's experimental maglev train sets a new world speed record of 361 mph (581 kph).

2004 China opens the Shanghai maglev line. Trains can reach 220 mph (350 kph) in two minutes.

2006 China opens the world's highest railroad, linking Beijing with Lhasa in Tibet, via Xining.

2006 The United States' Union Pacific Railroad sets a world record of 190 million tons of coal moved in one year.

2007 A specially designed French V150 TGV sets a new world record for electric traction of 356 mph (574 kph).

2007 Japan unveils its new N700 "green" bullet train, which delivers high-speed rail services with reduced energy use.

2018 First hydrogen-powered train enters service in northern Germany.

2020 China launches the first driverless bullet train, which runs between Beijing and Zhangjiakou, with a top speed of 217 mph (350 kph).

Find out more

Because trains are so popular, there is a wealth of places to go to discover more about railways. You can ride historic trains on a heritage railroad or visit transportation museums to see railroad artifacts. Your local library is likely to have railroad books, and you can search the internet for rail enthusiast groups, events, and special trains.

Goathland Station, North Yorkshire Moors Railway, UK

USEFUL WEBSITES

- Wikipedia has many articles about railroads, famous trains, and railroad history:
http://en.wikipedia.org/wiki/History_of_rail_transport
- Find out how locomotives, maglevs, and other rail technology works at How Stuff Works: **www.howstuffworks.com**
- The UK's National Railway Museum has online exhibitions, photo galleries, movie clips, and audio recordings:
www.railwaymuseum.org.uk
- The UK Heritage Railways site has technical details about locomotives, carriages, and signaling systems:
www.heritagerailways.com
- The National Railroad Museum of America tells the story of how rail shaped the US:
www.nationalrrmuseum.org
- The National Railway Historical Society is the main US umbrella group for all rail fans:
www.nrhs.com
- The website of the National Railway Museum in Port Adelaide, Australia, has online photo exhibitions of locomotives, carriages, rail cars, and stations:
www.natrailmuseum.org.au
- For details of how to travel by rail anywhere in the world, see:
www.seat61.com

Museum visits

Transportation museums usually have sections devoted to trains, and most countries have a national railroad museum. These are great places to get an overview of the development of trains and railroad technology.

Heritage railroads

Around the world there are many heritage railroads where you can still ride on steam trains and sometimes even get a lesson in how to drive a steam locomotive.

A steam locomotive at the Swiss Museum of Transportation, Lucerne, Switzerland.

Velorail in Brittany, France

Riding the rails

In some places, old disused railroad tracks have been turned into paths, allowing you to follow the routes once traveled by locomotives. In France, Sweden, Germany, and some other parts of Europe there are also velorails. Here you can pedal your own "carriage" over sections of preserved track no longer used by trains.

Harry Potter and the Chamber of Secrets (2002)

Snapping and spotting

Famous locomotives often come out on special occasions, giving rail enthusiasts a chance to photograph their favorite engines. "Train spotting" (collecting the numbers of engines still in service), is also a popular hobby among rail fans.

Microsoft®
Train Simulator
computer game

In the driver's seat

A train simulator is a video game that lets you experience what it's like to be in a locomotive's driving seat. This typically involves using the controls in a "virtual" cab to drive the train on a computerized representation of an actual route. More complex versions let you operate signals, and design your own routes.

PLACES TO VISIT

Baltimore & Ohio Railroad Museum, Baltimore, Maryland
The most comprehensive US collection of railroad exhibits.

Cité du Train, Mulhouse, France
The world-renowned French National Railway Museum houses many classic French locomotives.

National Railroad Museum, Green Bay, Wisconsin
Over 70 locomotives and rail cars, including *Big Boy*—the largest locomotive ever.

National Railway Museum, York, UK
The world's largest collection of trains and railroad artifacts, including Stephenson's original *Rocket* locomotive.

North Yorkshire Moors Railway, UK
The UK's most popular heritage steam railroad runs through beautiful moorland.

Science Museum, London, UK
Includes lots of exhibits on railroads, including *Puffing Billy* (1813).

State Railroad Museum, Sacramento, California
This tells the story of California's railroads and their impact on the "golden state."

Glossary

Diesel locomotive

AIR BRAKE A brake that relies on controlling air pressure to apply and release the brake.

BELL CODE A language for describing trains used by signalers to dispatch and receive trains.

BELL TAPPER A device used to tap out bell signals between signalers.

BLOCK A section of railroad controlled by a specific signaler or signal tower.

BOGIE A wheeled chassis or framework that is attached to a locomotive or train car by a swivel mounting.

BUFFER A shock absorber between rail vehicles.

BULLHEAD RAIL A type of rail developed in the UK, where the top half of the rail mirrors the bottom half. Once the running side was worn out, the rail was turned over and reused.

CAB The part of a locomotive from which the driver controls the train.

CABOOSE A rail vehicle that provides braking power for freight trains and accommodation for the train guard.

CARRIAGE A passenger vehicle on a train, also called a car (especially in North America).

CAST IRON A form of iron that can be cast, or molded, into almost any shape when molten. Cast iron was used to make rails and bridges in the early days of railroads. It was later replaced by stronger wrought iron.

Cast-iron emblem on a London railroad bridge

CHIMNEY The outlet on a steam locomotive through which the gases from the coal fire escape into the air.

CONTAINER A metal freight box that can be packed with goods and then transported by ships, trains, and trucks.

COUPLING The method of connecting rail vehicles together.

CRANK Part of a steam locomotive that transmits power from the piston to the driving wheels.

CUTTING A large ditch cut through the landscape to provide a more level route.

CYLINDER A chamber in an engine in which steam expands or fuel ignites to push pistons back and forth, generating power.

DIESEL LOCOMOTIVE A locomotive powered by a diesel engine.

DIESEL-ELECTRIC LOCOMOTIVE A locomotive with a diesel engine that produces power for electric traction motors, which drive the wheels.

DRIVING WHEEL A wheel that propels a locomotive along a track. On a steam locomotive, the driving wheels are powered by the pistons. On diesel and electric locomotives, electric motors supply power to the driving wheels.

ELECTRIC TRAIN A train that uses electricity from an external source—such as an overhead power line, third rail, or on-board batteries—to power traction motors on the train.

ELEVATED RAILROAD A railroad built on raised platforms through city streets, such as the former Liverpool Overhead Railway in the UK and part of the New York Subway in the US.

EMBANKMENT An earthen structure designed to raise a railroad above the natural ground level.

EXHAUST PIPE The pipe that allows waste gases from a diesel engine to escape.

FIREBOX A metal box in the heart of a steam locomotive, in which the fire is kept.

FIRE TUBE The fire tube conveys heat from a steam locomotive's fire to the boiler. This boils the water and makes steam.

FISH-BELLY RAIL A type of early cast-iron rail with a curved underside.

FLANGED WHEEL A train wheel with a metal lip called a flange on the inside edge.

FLAT-BOTTOMED RAIL The standard rail of today, which takes the form of a T-shape with a wide, flat base.

FREIGHT A term used to describe trains transporting finished goods and raw materials. It can also refer to the load itself.

FUNICULAR RAILWAY Used on tram, cliff, and industrial lines, funiculars use cables or chains to pull vehicles up and down slopes.

Funicular in Pau, France

GAUGE The measurement between the rails of a track. The world's most common gauge is 4 ft 8½ in (1,435 mm), and is known as standard gauge.

GAUGE GLASSES A device on a steam locomotive that shows the driver the level of water in the boiler. If the boiler were to run dry, the locomotive would explode.

HEADBOARD A notice on the front of a train that gives the train's name, route, or destination.

LEVEL CROSSING A place where a road crosses a railroad track on flat ground.

LOCOMOTIVE A self-propelled rail vehicle that can haul a train. There are steam, diesel, and electric locomotives.

MAGLEV TRAIN A train that works by being suspended and propelled over special tracks by electromagnetic force. Maglevs produce virtually no friction, and are very quiet.

MONORAIL A train that runs on a single rail.

OFF A signal is "off" when it is indicating that a train can proceed.

PISTON Part of a steam locomotive that drives the wheels. It consists of a rod inside a cylinder that is pushed in and out by steam. Other rods harness this motion and turn the wheels.

PLATE RAIL L-shaped iron rails used on plateways to guide cars with plain wheels. (Railroad vehicles today have flanged wheels.)

PLATEWAY An early railroad that used plate rail, often built as a feeder line to a canal or river.

POINTS Pieces of track that allow a train to switch from one set of tracks to another.

PULLMAN CAR A luxury train car for those who can pay a higher fare. Pullmans were introduced in the United States in 1865 as sleeping cars on long-distance trains, but the name later became synonymous with high-class rail travel.

RACK RAILROAD A railroad with an additional toothed rack-rail. The train or locomotive is fitted with a cog that links with the teeth on the rack-rail, enabling it to climb very steep slopes.

RAIL CAR A self-propelled passenger vehicle, usually with the engine located under the floor.

RAILROAD TIME Different places in the same country often had their own local time. In the 1840s, railroads began to introduce a standardized "railroad time" to avoid confusion caused by local time differences.

Rack railroad in Snowdonia, Wales

SHUNTER A small locomotive for moving trucks or wagons around a marshaling yard.

SIGNAL A fixed unit with an arm or a light that indicates whether a train should stop, go, or slow down. A signal also starts a train, whether it is by a whistle, hand gesture, or bell code.

SIGNAL BOX/SIGNAL TOWER A building in which the movement of trains is controlled by use of signals and coded messages sent from one signal box or tower to another.

Monorail at Walt Disney World in Florida

SLEEPER The cross-piece supporting the rails of a track, made out of wood, concrete, or steel.

SLEEPING CAR A train car with beds where passengers can sleep while traveling. Sleeping cars were first used in the United States in the 1830s.

STEAM LOCOMOTIVE A locomotive that generates steam by boiling water. The steam is then fed to cylinders that drive the wheels.

TAILLIGHT The lamp at the rear of a train. In the UK, a train is not complete without an illuminated rear warning light.

TANK ENGINE A steam engine that carries the water and coal it uses on the locomotive itself, rather than towing it behind in a tender.

TENDER The truck or wagon behind a steam locomotive that holds the locomotive's fuel and water.

TILTING TRAIN A train that can lean into bends, enabling it to travel faster along a route with many curves.

Loading rail trucks in Ghana

TOOTHED RAIL An additional rail often used on mountain railroads to enable a train to climb a steep hill (see Rack railroad).

TRAILING WHEEL An unpowered wheel located behind the driving wheels of a steam locomotive that provides support.

TRAIN An assembly of power unit and cars running on rails, carrying freight or passengers. If it is just the power unit, then it is a locomotive.

TRAIN FERRIES Ferries designed to take rail vehicles by having a deck with tracks.

TRUCK A small rail wagon.

VACUUM BRAKE A type of brake that is held off by a partial vacuum, and applied when air is let into the system.

WAGON A rail vehicle for carrying freight.

WROUGHT IRON A form of iron that is worked by being forged or hammered, and which was used before the invention of steel.

Index

Acknowledgments

The publisher would like to thank the following people for their help with making the book: Staff at the National Railway Museum, York, especially David Wright and Richard Gibbon; John Liffen at the Science Museum; Justin Scobie for photographic assistance; The London Transport Museum; the signal box staff of Three Bridges (British Rail) Station, West Sussex; The Bluebell Railway; Gatwick Airport; Robert Gwynne and Russell Hollowood at the National Rail Museum, York, for assisting with updates; Claire Gillard for initial research; Rupa Rao, Helena Spiteri, Lisa Stock, and Gin von Noorden for editorial assistance; Earl Neish for design assistance; Vijay Kandwal for color work; Priyanka Sharma-Saddi for the jacket; Ann Baggaley for proofreading; and Elizabeth Wise for the index.

The publisher would like to thank the following for their kind permission to reproduce their photographs:
(Key: a-above; b-below/bottom; c-center; f-far; l-left; r-right; t-top)
Advertising Archives: 26bc; **Alamy Images:** 33tc, Artepics Bridgeman Images 30cb, Anthony Brown 49ca, Bradley Caslin 47cla, Historic Collection 29tr, Jerry Tavin / Everett Collection 25tr, The Print Collector 8tr, Alex Fairweather 7cra, FineArt 13cra, ILYA GENKIN 23bc, Dennis Schmelz / Mauritius images GmbH 43l, Paul Heinrich 52–53c, Science History Images 41tr, World History Archive 42bc, imageBROKER 58–59tl, J3BJP4 59tr, Niday Picture Library 36tl, Ben McRae 47tr, Granger, NYC 19crb, Granger, NYC. 39tr, eye35.pix 49br, Dave Porter 6–7t, Qaphotos.com 21clb, Christoph Rueegg 41cr, Steve Tulley 63bl, Asar Studios 11ca, Daniel Wyre 53tc, Zoonar / zhang zhiwei 33b; Steve Crise / Transtock Inc. 62–63c; Michael Grant 70lb; JTB Photo Communications, Inc. 65bl, 65tl; James Lovell 68tl; Iain Masterton 67br; Sami Sarkis France 69tl; Nick Suydam 64cla.
alimdi.net: Photographers Direct 68br. **Aquarius Library:** Warner Bros 69tr. **Australian Overseas Information Service, London:** 42tr. **Barlow Reid:** 41cl. **Bettmann Archive / Hulton Picture Library:** 19t. **Bridgeman Art Library / Science**

Museum, London: 11btc; National Railway Museum, York 11tr; Private Collections: 13btc; Guildhall Library, Corporation of London: 56cl. **Bridgeman Images:** Peter Newark American Pictures 18tl. **Britt Allcroft (Thomas Ltd), 1989:** 61tr. **Jean-Loup Charmet:** 10cra, 30bl, 39bl, 44cl, 56tr. **J.A. Coiley:** 54cr, 58br. **Corbis:** Eleanor Bentall 65br; Ursula Gahwiler / Robert Harding World Imagery 64tr; Colin Garratt, Milepost 92 _ 71cr; Gavin Hellier / Robert Harding World Imagery 67cl; Dave G. Houser 64bc; Bruno Morandi / Robert Harding World Imagery 65tc; Michael Reynolds / EPA 65tr; Phil Schermeister 64bl; Naoaki Watanabe / amanaimages 65cr; Culver Pictures Inc.: 11tl, 16btr, 19br, 37tl, 41btr. **DK Images:** Rough Guides 71ct, 71bl. **Docklands Light Railway Ltd / Marysha Alwan:** 62tl. **drr. net:** Joern Sackermann 69bc. **e.t. archive:** 6bl, 9cl, 9tc, 9c, 12cra, 16bl, 20tr, 26btr (detail), 28cr, 29ca, 32tr, 46cl, 49bca, 51tr. **Getty Images:** Construction Photography / Avalon 46–47b, Bettmann 20cb, Franck Chazot 58clb, Print Collector 21cra, Mike Danneman 26–27t, FatCamera 61b, Science & Society Picture Library 9tr, Science & Society Picture Library 15tc, Science & Society Picture Library Bridgeman Images 12–13b, Prakash Singh 57clb, Paolo Vieceli 35clb; Hulton Archive / Andrew Joseph Russell / MPI 66br. **Getty Images / iStock:** ZU_09 42cl. **Hulton Picture Company:** 31btl. **Hutchison Picture Library:** 53acr. **Antony J. Lambert:** 45c, 60car. **La vie du rail, Paris:** 39ca, 39tl. **Mack Sennet Productions:** 25acr. **Mansell Collection Ltd:** 23. **Mary Evans Picture Library:** 8br, 9cr, 12t, 17btl, 21cr, 28cl, 41tr, 61acl. **John Massey Stewart:** 45bcl, 59tl. **Microsoft:** Microsoft product screen shot reprinted with permission from Microsoft Corporation 69c. **Millbrook House Ltd:** 7abl, 22br, 37br, 51btl, 58acl, 63tr. **National Railway Museum:** 6cl, 6cr, 13btr, 21tc, 21tr, 22bc, 25cr, 25bcr, 26cr, 30bc, 35cr, 37btr, 43bcr, 49tl, 50cr, 59cr; Terence Cuneo: 33c. **PA Photos:** DPA Deutsche Press-Agentur / DPA 62br. **Peter Newark's Picture Library:** 13cr, 18cr, 19c, 19tr, 24acr, 34tl, 42crb, 43br, 53cr. **Quadrant Picture Library:** 27btc, 43crb, 53crb. **Rank Films:** 49cl. **Retrograph Archive / Martin Breese:** 37cr. **Robert Harding Picture Library:** 52cl,

58bl. **Telegraph Colour Library:** 50tr, 57c. **Weintraub / Ronald Grant:** 31tl. **Zefa Picture Library:** 24tl, 35tl, 59b. **University of Birmingham:** 63br; **Dreamstime.com:** Richie Chan 22–23c. **Science Photo Library:** Maertin Bond 63tl. **University of Pittsburgh:** 35br.

All other images © Dorling Kindersley
For further information see:
www.dkimages.com